Text

Building skills in English

BOOK 2

Annabel Charles • Sam Custance
David Grant • Julia Hubbard • Esther Menon
Consultant: Cindy Torn

www.heinemann.co.uk
✓ Free online support
✓ Useful weblinks
✓ 24 hour online ordering

01865 888118

Contents

Text: Building Skills in English 11-14

1 Advertising

Objectives

In this unit you will:

Reading

- make notes on and summarise the main points of a range of texts
- read a range of texts and identify their purpose and target audience
- comment on how the writer's language choices and techniques help persuade the reader
- explore and analyse how texts are designed for effect, including the use of colour, fonts, images and layout.

Composition

- plan different types of writing, using evidence to make your meaning clear
- write a range of different forms of adverts for different audiences, using persuasive language and techniques for effect.

Conventions

- understand when formal and informal language is appropriate and put this to use in your own writing
- understand the use of prepositions, connectives and the different types of clauses and sentences and use them in your own writing.

Speaking and listening

- Plan and give a presentation in which the structure and language persuade the audience.

By the end of this unit you will:

- prepare a presentation to persuade a company to produce and sell your product (Speaking and Listening: Speaking and presenting)
- write a letter to the council arguing that the local community centre should be kept open (Writing: Composition and conventions).

Cross-curricular links

- **Citizenship**
Critical thinking and enquiry; Advocacy and representation

w attraction

...ple Planet
...om 0-90 will love our
...interactive zone
...s state-of-the-art
...y. See yourself
...red in virtual
...colate rain, stare in
...zement as your
...ge is re-created
...chocolate and
...hase runaway
...bury Creme Eggs!

...sence
...w the signs
...e yellow
...prints to the
...ear of Cadbury World
...to discover Essence. Travel back
...in time to witness the creation of
...Cadbury Dairy Milk. Create your
...own unique Cadbury concoction
...by choosing a filling from popcorn to
...arshmallows. Warm liquid chocolate
...dded to your cup of goodies for the
...ost delicious taste sensation.

CILLIT BANG

1 What is advertising?

You are learning:

● to recognise the purposes of advertising and the effect it has on its target audience.

Advertising is the way in which businesses try to persuade people to buy their product or service. It gives people information and tries to make people want to buy that product or service. Advertising might highlight a product, such as a new pair of trainers; or a service, such as a DVD rental company.

Activity 1

Advertisers use different media to reach the public; for example television, the internet, magazines and newspapers. The choice of media depends on:

● the purpose of the advertising
● the target audience
● how much money the advertisers have to spend on marketing their product.

Different media reach different groups of people. Match the different media below to their likely target audiences by copying out the words and joining them up with lines. An example is done for you.

	Type of media		Target audience
1	UK motorway service station billboard	a	the world
2	leaflets available in all UK tourist information offices	b	local people
3	worldwide superstore's website	c	UK teenagers
4	teen magazine	d	car users
5	London Underground subway billboard	e	local shoppers
6	teen Weight Wise's website	f	UK teenage girls
7	the *Local Times* newspaper	g	tourists from the UK and abroad
8	Bob the butcher's high-street shop window	h	Londoners and tourists

Activity 2

1   Look at the list of products and services below.
    a   Which media would you **not** use for each of the products or services?
    b   Which would be a good media form?

Product or service
- a new Italian restaurant
- a new computer game launched by a large computer game manufacturer
- information for the elderly about winter fuel payments available
- information about a 'Paint your own Pottery' activity studio
- a new ice cream parlour

Media form
- company website
- national newspaper
- teenage girls' magazine
- fliers delivered to local houses
- TV advert in a specific time slot on a commercial TV channel
- local radio advert
- billboards on motorways and at motorway service stations
- billboards at bus stops
- posters in local schools and nurseries

Here is an example:

THE MAIL

Tuesday 12th February 2008

SANTELLA

New Italian restaurant opening in Ramsley

Come and try our range of home-cooked Italian dishes

10% off with this flier for first-time customers visiting between 5th & 12th April

This would be a very expensive way of reaching a lot of people when you only need local people.

This is a way of reaching all people in your local area, as most people will pick up their post.

c Use a table like the one below to write down your ideas for each product or service.

Write a sentence or two to explain each of your choices.

Product or service	Purpose of advert	An unsuccessful way to advertise	A good way to advertise	Why this is a good way to advertise
A new Italian restaurant	To encourage customers to visit the restaurant	National newspapers	Fliers delivered to local houses	The restaurant needs to attract customers from the local area
A new computer game launched by a large computer game manufacturer	To increase sales of the game			
Information for the elderly about winter fuel payments available	To encourage the elderly to get the benefits to which they are entitled			
Information about a 'Paint your own Pottery' activity studio	To encourage parents and children to do the activities			
A new ice cream parlour	To encourage customers to visit the parlour			

Sharpen your skills Prepositions

Read these sentences:

He jumped <u>onto</u> the wall.

He fell <u>off</u> the wall.

The underlined words are prepositions. They come before a noun phrase and give information about time, place and direction.

You need to be able to recognise prepositions and use them in your own writing.

1 Make a list of all the prepositions in the pottery advert below.

Country Crafts Pottery
Baby Hand- and Footprint Glazing

Have babies' hand- or footprints glazed onto plates, mugs, trinket boxes, etc.

Ideal presents to wrap up for Christmas!

Book our mobile unit to come into your toddler group, pre-school group or nursery.

Paint your own designs onto plates or mugs by coming into our studio after school or at weekends at 29 Rudd Street, Asthall.

2 Write your own advert for a new local dry ski slope. Make sure your advert contains at least three prepositions.

2 Persuasive language

You are learning:
● to identify examples of persuasive language in advertisements and to understand their effect on the audience.

The main purpose of advertising is to persuade. This is done through the use of persuasive language – the words used in advertising try to persuade the audience to do something.

Activity 1

The advert opposite is designed to tempt people to visit Cadbury World in Birmingham.

1 Identify the following persuasive features in the advert:
   ● Emotional words that appeal to the audience's feelings, for example, *We're **desperate** for your help.*
   ● Imperative verbs that tell the reader to do something, for example, *Make a difference.*
   ● Phrases that give readers a reason for buying, for example, *Be beautiful!*
   ● Words such as *you*, *your* and *we* that involve the reader, for example, *We look forward to seeing you.*
   ● Opinions and positive language to make the product look good, for example, *It's easy, beautiful, high quality.*

2 Write a sentence or two about each of the features you identified, explaining the effect the writer wanted to have on the reader. Use this example to help you:

'Kids from 0–90 will love our newest...' The writer uses the word 'love' because it is a positive word with emotional appeal which emphasises how much the audience will enjoy themselves.

Activity 2

1 A slogan is a short, catchy phrase or sentence that tries to sum up the appeal of a product or service. Slogans are aimed at the target audience of the product or service. Look at these examples:

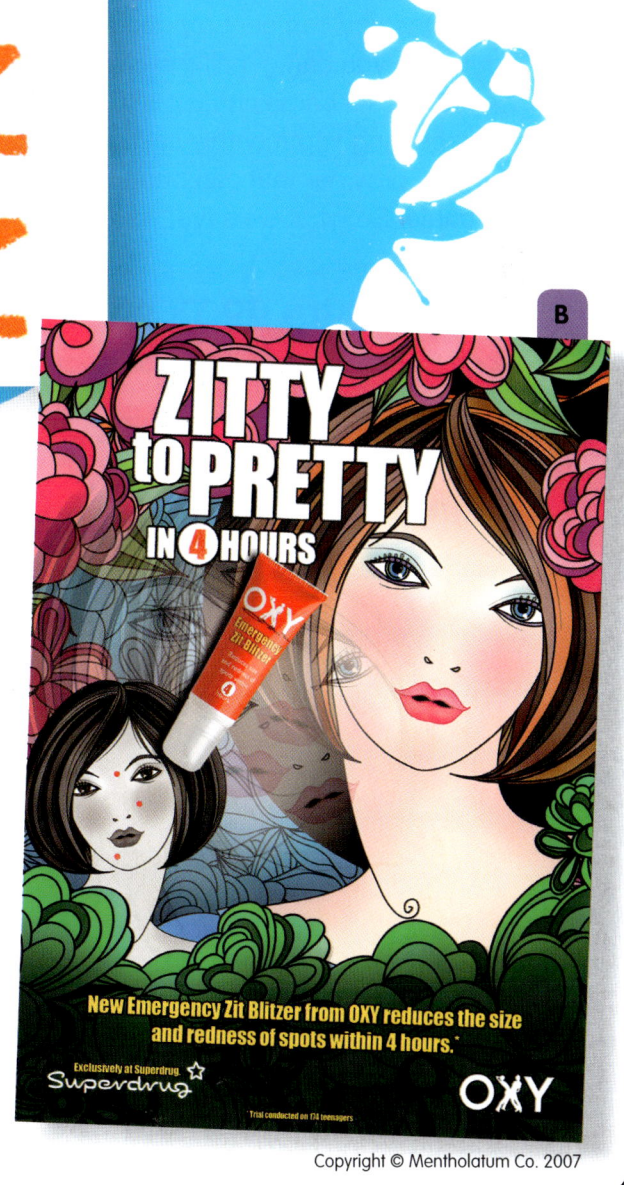

2 a Who is the target audience for each of these slogans?
b How did you make your decision about who the target audience is?

3 How have the writers of these slogans made them memorable and appealing to their target audience?

4 Write a slogan to sell a new mobile phone to a target audience of teenagers. Try to use some of the persuasive features you identified in Activity 1.

5 What would you need to change in your slogan to sell the mobile phone to a target audience of over-60s? Why would your original slogan not appeal to this new audience?

Activity 3

A direct mail is an advert in the form of a letter sent directly to a person without them asking for it. Read the example of a direct mail below.

TalkBritain

Ms Jennifer Hawkins
23 Wool Lane
Liverpool
L17 4BC

Broadband, phone and digital TV: 3 for £30!

Dear Ms Hawkins,

Of course you can get broadband, phone and digital TV separately, but why would you when you can get all three services together from TalkBritain, for just £30 a month? It's a bargain that could save you £100 a year! With TalkBritain you'll make genuine, ongoing monthly savings. That's because, unlike Sky, BT and AOL, we're the only provider that can bring all three services into the home via *one* state-of-the art cable. So what we save, you save!

And an extra 60 TV channels FREE in the first month!

For a limited time only if you order our £30 digital TV, broadband and phone services bundle package, we'll give you a FREE upgrade to our digital TV Family Pack. That means you can enjoy over 60 channels of fantastic digital TV, worth £8.50, for FREE for the first month!

Call our switchline now on 0800 011 324 and we'll give you free installation worth £75, together with a 30-day money back guarantee. That's how confident we are that you'll be happier when you switch to TalkBritain.

Call and start saving today!

Yours sincerely,

James Jenkins

James Jenkins
Marketing Director

Get set for digital ☑

1   Make a list of all the benefits Ms Hawkins will enjoy if she buys this service.

2   TalkBritain could have advertised this service on billboards or on the television. Why do you think they have chosen to use direct mail?

3   Find an example of a direct address to the reader using the second person: 'you'. What effect does this have on the reader?

4   Find two examples of positive language (words or phrases that tell the reader how good the product is).

5   Find two phrases that include imperatives, for example 'Buy this' and 'Act now'. What effect does this have on the reader?

6   Advertisers sometimes use what people want or worry about to persuade them to buy a product, for example:

Explanation

imperative a command or order

worry
germs causing harm

product
household cleaning product

want
up-to-date gadgets

product
latest mobile phone

Which of the readers' worries or wants is being used to attract them to the products in the letter on page 12?

beauty

getting a bargain

happiness

glamour

happy families

Assess your progress

Look back at your answers to Activities 1 and 2. Use the table below to select the level that best reflects your work.

Level 4	Level 5	Level 6
I can identify persuasive words the writer has chosen to use	I can explain why a writer might have chosen particular words	I can explain in detail the significance of particular words
I can say why one word is better than another	I can suggest possible effects on the reader of particular words	I can comment in detail on the effects on the reader of particular words

Set yourself a target for when you next write about a writer's use of language.

Target: when I am commenting on writers' use of language my target is to …

3 Colourful copy

You are learning:

- to recognise how descriptive language is used in adverts to make a product more appealing.

While pictures are crucial to many adverts, advertisers also use language to create a picture in our minds. The author of a novel or short story might use adjectives, adverbs and figurative language to create a setting and atmosphere. Advertisers use the same techniques to help us imagine a product and its benefits and to make us want to buy it.

Activity 1

Holiday companies often use words to create a picture in their adverts. This helps potential customers to imagine themselves at the resort and encourages them to book a holiday.

1   Read this webpage from UK Center Parcs holiday resorts. The target audience is families with adults and children who have various holiday needs, from adventure and excitement to relaxation.

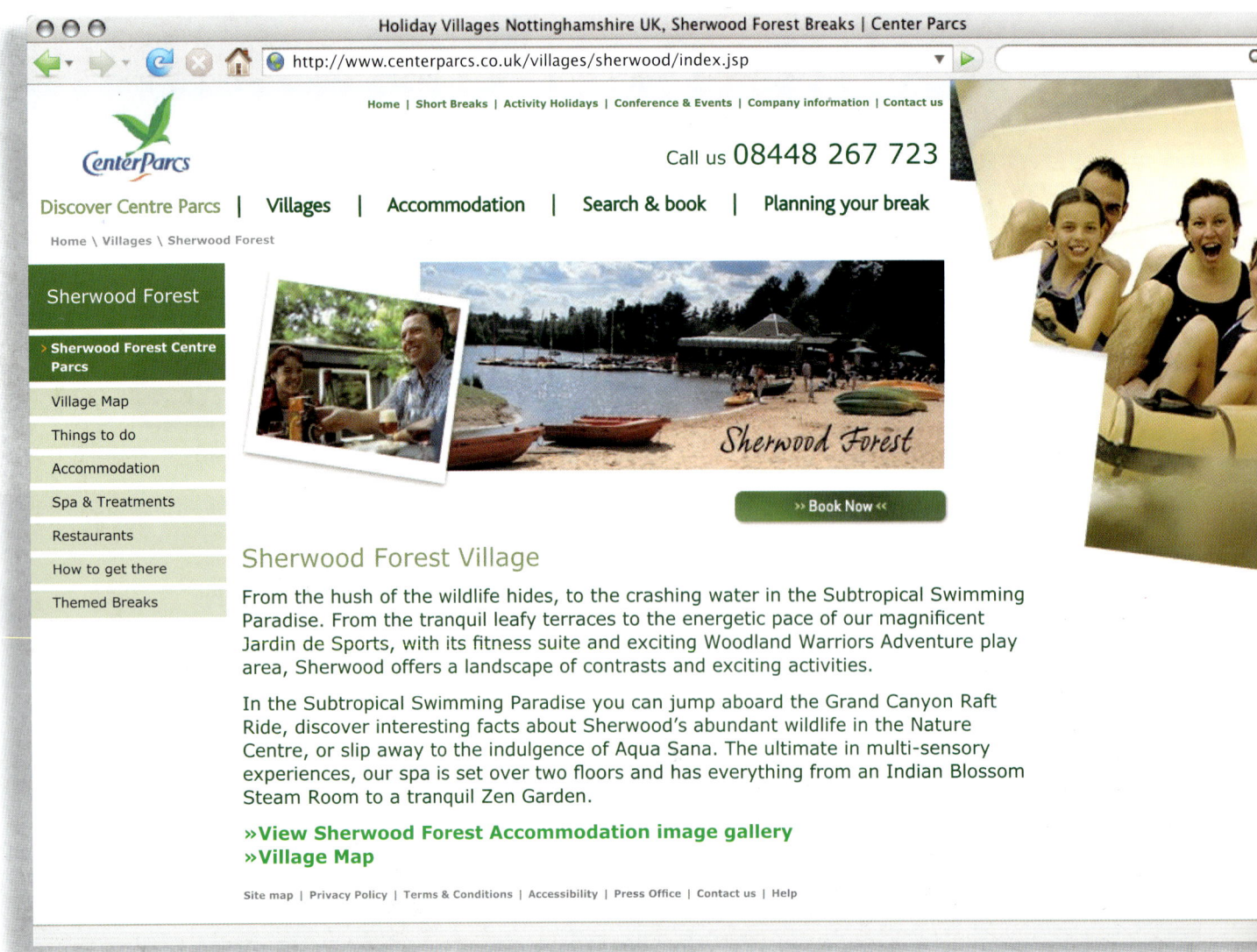

a Choose five powerful adjectives from the webpage that you think create a persuasive picture. For each adjective, write a comment explaining what you think the writer is trying to suggest. An example has been done for you.

'Crashing water' – suggests that the water is exciting

b Write down the names given to the different areas of this resort. What does each of them suggest about the place?

'Subtropical Swimming Paradise' – tells us there is a swimming pool, but it also suggests that it is warm by the use of the word 'subtropical' and beautiful with the word 'paradise'.

Sharpen your skills Clauses

A clause is a group of words containing a subject and verb. There are different types of clauses.

- A main clause makes sense on its own.
- A subordinate clause relies on the main clause to make sense.
- A simple sentence contains one clause.

Read the numbered phrases below and identify which ones are main clauses. Then try to make as many sentences as possible using the main and subordinate clauses below. The first one has been done for you as an example.

1 the opening of the restaurant was a resounding success
        └── main clause

- Although he had been worried, the opening of the restaurant was a resounding success.
- Since people were asking for organic products, the opening of the restaurant was a resounding success.
- The opening of the restaurant was a resounding success, since people were asking for organic products.

2 the butcher was widening his business
3 the florist was extremely worried
4 because of the floods in the shop
5 although he had been worried
6 since people were asking for organic products

4 Visual language

You are learning:
● to understand the effect of advertising images on audience.

Advertisers choose their images carefully to help get their message across. To read and analyse TV and film adverts we have to think about the positioning of the images, the setting, what the people are wearing and their body language. All these elements combine to get the advertisers' message across.

Activity 1

1 Read the advert from Cancer Research UK.

a What is the purpose of the advert?

b How does the language used persuade the reader to take part? Look at the persuasive features on page 10 if you need help.

CANCER RESEARCH UK 10K
Blenheim Palace
Sunday 30th September at 10am

Join hundreds from Oxfordshire and run 10k for Cancer Research UK at Blenheim Palace this autumn. Running 10k is a great way to get fit and by raising sponsorship money for Cancer Research UK's groundbreaking research too, you will be helping more people beat cancer in the future. Places are limited so register now at www.cancerresearchuk10.co.uk.

2 Look carefully at the images.
a What does each image suggest about the kind of people who take part in the run?
b How do the images help to persuade the reader to take part?

This image suggests that the run is fun as both people are smiling. It might also suggest that the run is for all types of people of different levels of fitness as neither the man or woman are young and the man isn't very athletic.

Activity 2

1 Three different fonts are used in this advert for After Eight bags. Write a sentence or two about each font, explaining why the designer chose to use them.

2 Look at the colours the designer has chosen for this advert.

   a Why do you think the bags are different colours?

   b What does the gold colour suggest about the product?

   c Why has the designer chosen a dark green background?

   d How would it change the advert's message if the background was yellow or orange?

3 Imagine that the company wanted to show a model in this advert. Write a description of the model that you would use, what he or she might be wearing and the setting in which they and the product might be placed.

Assess your progress

Choose an advert and analyse it in the same way you did with the After Eight advert.

1 Think carefully about the following issues:
- What is being advertised?
- Who do you think is the target audience?
- What do the advertisers want the audience to do?
- How do the images appeal to the audience?
- How does the setting or background of the advert appeal to the audience?
- How have colour and font been used?
- What persuasive techniques can you see in the language used?

Explain to a partner how each of these aspects works to persuade the intended audience.

2 Rate your confidence in identifying and commenting on the images, or visual language, in the adverts.

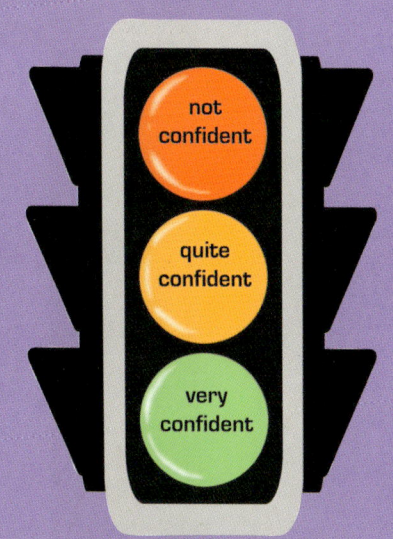

5 Target audience

Advertisers need to identify the particular people they are trying to persuade before designing their adverts. This target audience will influence their choices of text and design.

Activity 1

1 Look at the following webpages.

a Identify the product or service that is being advertised and the specific target audience of each webpage.

b Look carefully at images, colour, layout, font and language to help you reach an answer. Make notes and record your answers in a table like the one on page 19. Remember to give reasons why you think the website designer made these choices.

webpage A

webpage B

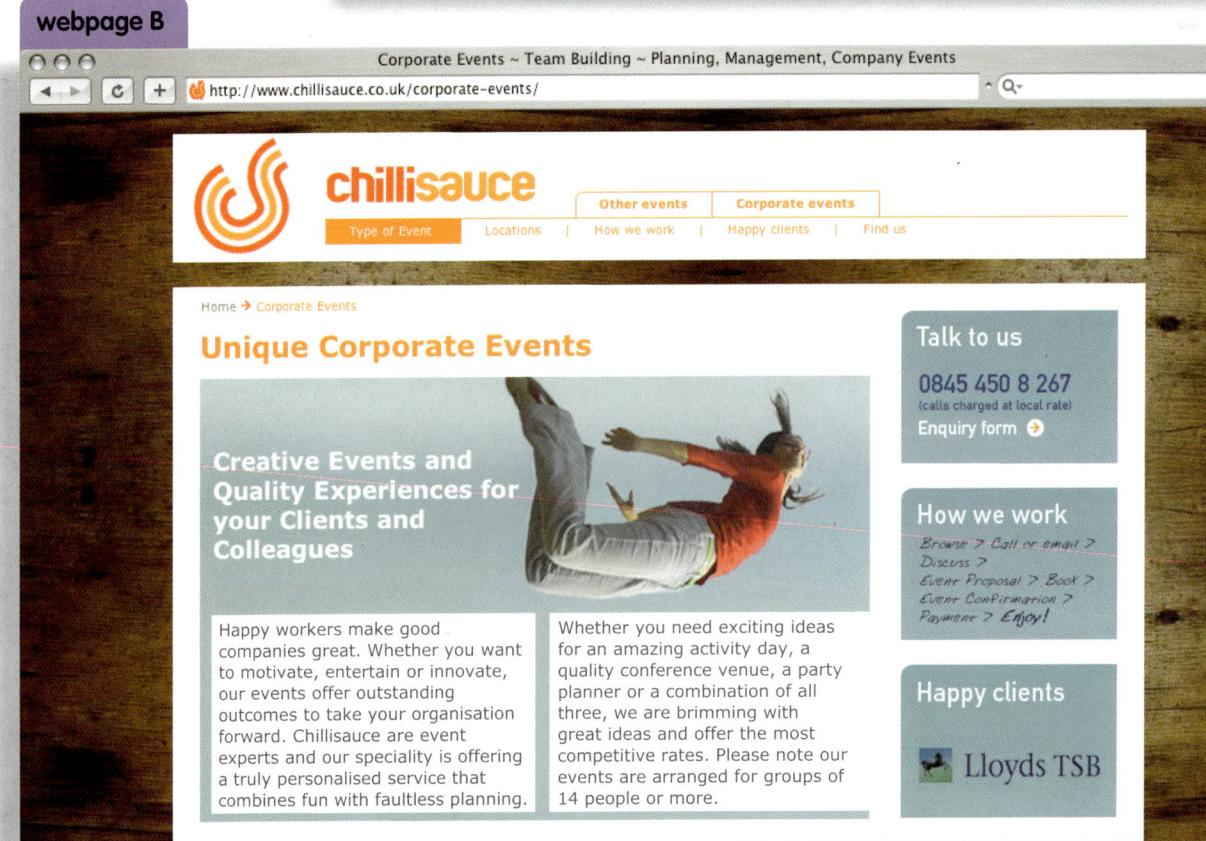

webpage C

Seniors Transportation with Driving Miss Daisy

http://www.drivingmissdaisy.net/

Getting Started   Latest Headlines

Driving Miss Daisy
Ride with a friend, not a stranger

December 12, 2007   Home   About Us   Franchise Opportunities   ▼   Media   Links

Contact Us
Our Services
Special Needs
Rates

Welcome To Driving Miss Daisy

Driving Miss Daisy is a seniors' transportation, assistance and accompaniment service that commenced service on January 1, 2002 in St. Albert, Alberta Canada with 1 car and has since expanded to 18 cars. These cars are operated by owner/operators who have purchased franchises in the City of Edmonton, St. Albert, Sherwood Park, Spruce Grove, Devon, Fort Saskatchewan, Millet and Wetaskiwin.

Each Franchisee offers safe, reliable transportation, assistance and accompaniment to anywhere their senior clients need to go including:

Medical Appointments	Shopping
Hair Salon	Airport
Adult Day Programs	Dialysis Units
Alzheimer's Companion	Social Events Accompaniment
Vacation Accompaniment	

The Franchisees invite you to 'Ride with a friend, not a stranger' and let them accompany you to a fuller life!

Gift certificates are available and are the perfect gift for your loved ones.

Testimonial #1

"I love my Daisy, Colette, because she is always willing to help me with my wheelchair and is always on time."

Done

webpage D

Sheilas' Wheels – Women's car insurance

http://www.sheilaswheels.com/

Car Insurance   Home Insurance

Welcome to Sheilas' Wheels

Car Insurance

- With handbag cover up to £300
- Female friendly repairers

Get a quote now

Find out more

Already a customer?

Retrieve a quote

We don't just do wheels...

Home Insurance

- Pest cover option available
- Home Emergency option available

Get a quote

Find out more

VeriSign

Find out more   •   Buyers guide   •   About Sheilas' Wheels   •   Media centre   •   Small print   •   FAQs   •   Contact us

Webpage	Product or service	Target audience	Why the image was chosen	Why the colours were chosen	Why this layout was chosen
A	motorbikes	women	the image of the bike makes it seem large, powerful, shiny and glamorous	a strong, rich colour to reflect the product and its audience	the image and the text are large, dominating the page and grabbing the reader's attention
B					

Activity 2

1   Look carefully at the flier below and answer the following
    questions. Use what you have learned so far about audience,
    purpose and advertising techniques.
    a   Who is the target audience of this advert?
    b   What is the purpose of the advert?

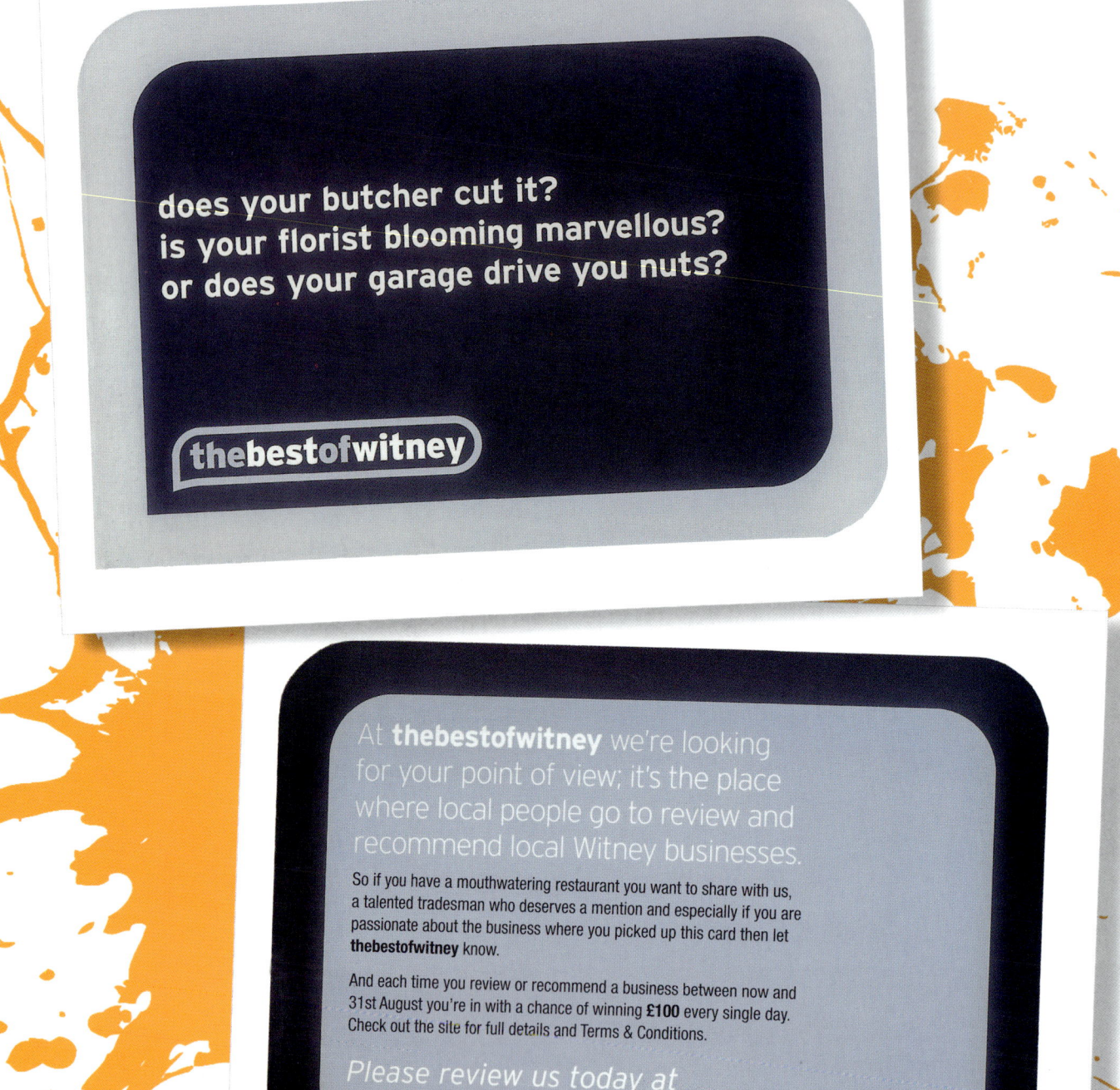

2 Write two paragraphs identifying and explaining the persuasive techniques in the advert: one about language and one about colour, font and layout. Look back at the list of persuasive features on page 10 to help you. Remember to use evidence to support your answer.

3 Suggest three ways of improving this advert and give reasons for your answers.
For example:

> • The text of '£100' could be in a different colour to grab the reader's attention.

Sharpen your skills Compound and complex sentences

A compound sentence is two simple sentences joined together with a connective such as *and*, *but*, *or*, *so*. Each simple sentence must make sense on its own.

For example:

I helped my friend **and** she passed her science test.

simple sentence   connective   simple sentence

compound sentence

1 Complete these sentences about a trip to Center Parcs to make compound sentences.
  a I enjoyed the Jardin de Sport but…
  b My mother hated the adventure play area and…
  c You can travel by car or…

A complex sentence is made up of a main clause and a subordinate clause. The subordinate clause needs to be joined to the main clause to make sense. The subordinate clause can go before or after the main clause.

I enjoy art because I'm good at it.

For example:

I enjoy art **because I'm good at it.**

main clause   subordinate clause

means the same as:
Because I'm good at it, I enjoy art.

2 Complete these sentences to make complex sentences:
  a The name of the spa area seemed ridiculous since…
  b When you travel to Center Parcs,…
  c David didn't enjoy the swimming because…

Assessment task

Speaking and Listening: Speaking and presenting

We know you're going to like it...

You are a young, dynamic design group who have developed a brand new product aimed at the teenage market. It could be a snack bar, a sports drink, a fashion accessory or a technological item such as a new kind of mobile phone.

Your task

Big Company Ltd is looking for exciting and innovative products to produce and sell. You have the chance to persuade them that they want to produce **your** product. They will want to know why your product will sell and how you will advertise it.

Prepare a presentation to persuade the company to produce and sell your product. Use this flow chart to help you.

1 Choose your product

What **product** are you going to create?

Remember: It must be aimed at a teenage market.

What **special features** will make your product more appealing to teenagers than other similar products?

2 Design two magazine adverts for your product

a Choose a **name** for your product.

Remember: The name needs to suggest what your product is and why it's so special.

b Create a **logo** for your product.

Think carefully about the font you will use for the name of your product. Choose colours that appeal to teenagers.

c Decide how your two adverts will differ.

They could show your product in two different situations to show how versatile it is.

For example, they could appeal to both boys and girls.

3 Plan your presentation

What are you going to tell the people at Big Company Ltd to persuade them to produce your product?

Make a list of the different things you will tell them about. **Organise** them into sections. **Number** your sections to show in what order you will explain them.

d Plan how you will sell the product in your advert.

How will you make the target audience realise that they cannot live without your product?

e Select the **colours** you will use in your advert.

Which colours best show your target audience what your product is like? Is it sophisticated and expensive? Fun and exciting? Mysterious and magical?

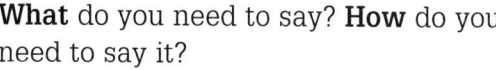

4 Prepare your presentation

Who will say **what** in the presentation?

Decide who is going to present the different sections.

f Select the **font** you will use in your advert.

Is your product for special occasions only? For everyday use? Tough and long-lasting? Or something else?

5 Practise your presentation

What do you need to say? **How** do you need to say it?

You can make notes to help you give your presentation, but don't write your presentation down and then read it out!

Practise your presentation, making sure that everyone knows what to say and when to say it.

Help your group by suggesting things you could say or do.

g Select the **model** or **models** you will use in your advert.

What will they wear? What are they doing? How are they standing or sitting?

Remember: Your models should be like your target audience and should suggest the effect your product will have.

6 Give your presentation

h Do a rough **draft** of your advert.

You can use arrows and labels to suggest some of your decisions about models, colour, font etc.

Remember: You need to **give** your presentation, not read it aloud!

Look at the audience, be persuasive and sound like you mean it.

Good luck!

6 Developing an argument

Advertising tries to persuade us to buy something. Lots of other kinds of texts try to change our minds and shape our opinions. The writers of these texts often use an argument – a series of points or ideas – to convince the audience that their opinion is the right one.

Activity 1

1 Look at the two texts: text A is an advert for a youth festival and text B is an argument written to a local newspaper from a parent.

A

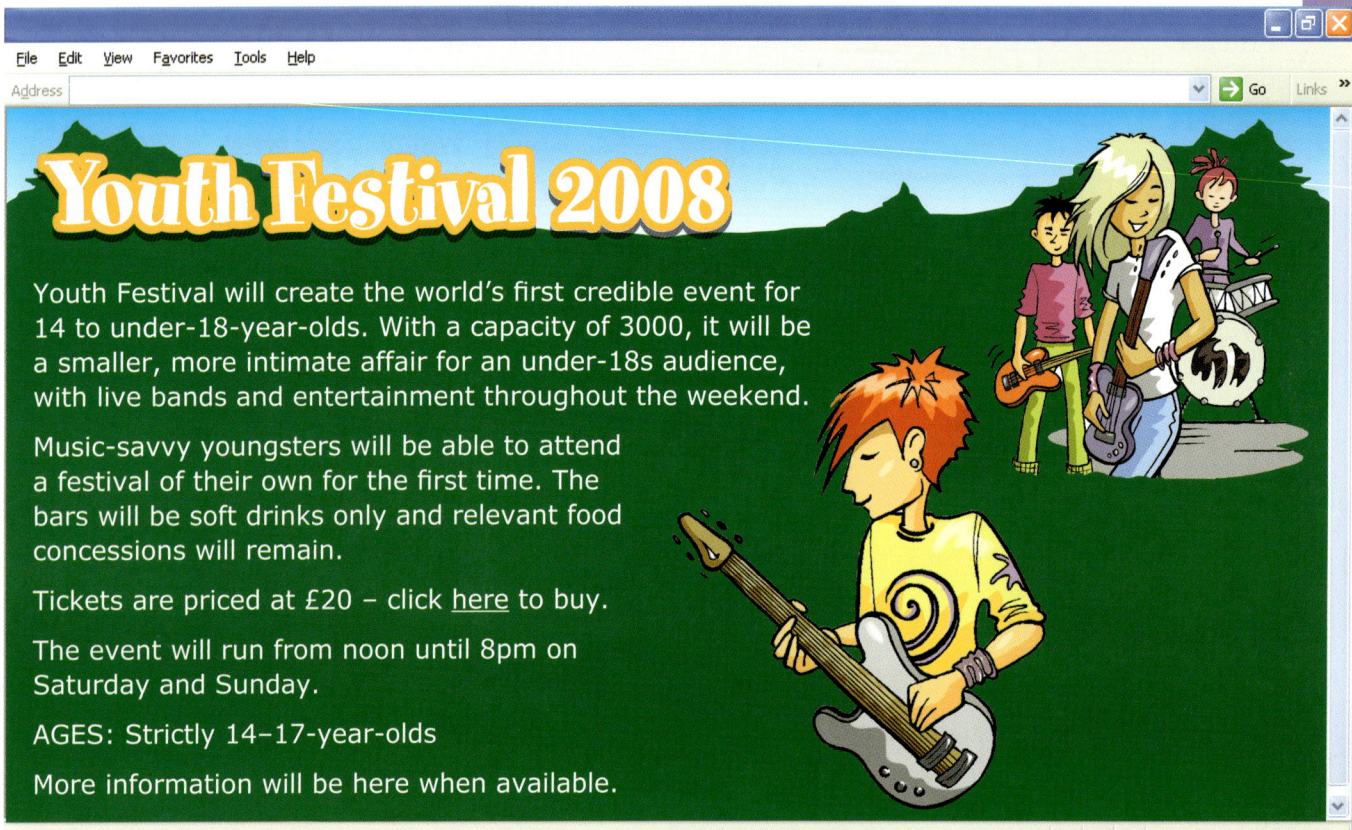

Youth Festival 2008

Youth Festival will create the world's first credible event for 14 to under-18-year-olds. With a capacity of 3000, it will be a smaller, more intimate affair for an under-18s audience, with live bands and entertainment throughout the weekend.

Music-savvy youngsters will be able to attend a festival of their own for the first time. The bars will be soft drinks only and relevant food concessions will remain.

Tickets are priced at £20 – click here to buy.

The event will run from noon until 8pm on Saturday and Sunday.

AGES: Strictly 14–17-year-olds

More information will be here when available.

B

Dear Sir/Madam,

I am disgusted to see details of a new festival aimed at teenagers taking place in Stratford this summer. We continue to push our teenagers to grow up too quickly. Teenagers are being forced to become more and more sophisticated. They are pressurised to behave like adults. No doubt this event will encourage children into violence, alcohol and drugs. Let children be children, and leave clubbing and festival-going for adults. These events pressurise parents to allow their children to venture far from the safety of their family.

Yours faithfully

R. Hughes, Stratford

2 Summarise the main points that the parent makes in text B.

3   Imagine that you are the organiser of the festival. How would you respond to text B? What arguments would you use against the parent's main points?

a   Children are pushed to grow up too quickly.

b

c

WHY OUR TOWN SHOULD HAVE A YOUTH FESTIVAL

FESTIVAL

3

2

1

Activity 2

1   Using the planning staircase on the right, organise your points to argue the case for running a youth festival in your own town. Each step should build up your case for running the festival with a group of your friends.

2   Check that your points are in the best order for making your case.

3   Add some evidence to support each of your points. This could be a fact or statistic, or something from your own experience, for example:

To support this point…

If young people had something good to do – like going to this festival – maybe it would prevent us from behaving antisocially.

…you could use this statistic as evidence:

A recent survey revealed that teenagers behave antisocially when they are bored.

…or you could use this personal experience:

I know lots of people who go to festivals and none of them drink or take drugs.

Sharpen your skills Connectives

- Connectives join words, phrases or simple sentences together
- Connectives can add information
- Connectives can show contrast.

Look back at the parent's main points in Activity 1.

1   Use connectives from the table to link two statements together extending your points of argument.

2   Use connectives to join your own statements with the parent's to allow you to dismiss their points using contrast. Add extra words where this helps you express your points clearly. For example:

Adding	Contrast
and	although
similarly	whereas
in the same way	however
also	in contrast

The writer of this letter argues that we should let children be children. However, this does not mean that children have to sit at home all weekend doing nothing!

7 Formal and informal language

You are learning:
- to tell the difference between informal and formal language and understand when each is appropriate.

Writers use formal or informal language in a text depending on their audience and purpose. If you were arguing your case with a parent, you might use informal language. However, if you were writing a letter arguing your case to someone you did not know, you should choose formal language. In order to win your argument, it is important to choose the level of formality suitable to your audience.

Activity 1

Look at texts A–F below.

1   Which texts would you expect to be written in a formal style and which in an informal style? Label each one *informal* or *formal*.

2   For each one write a sentence or two explaining why you think this is so.

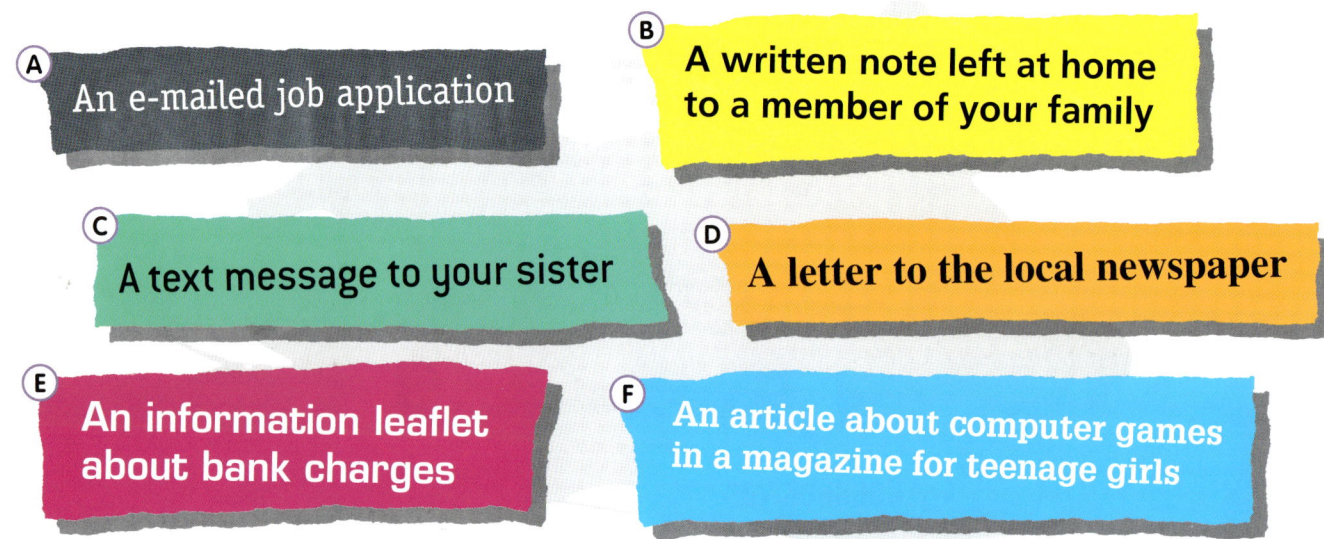

A   An e-mailed job application

B   A written note left at home to a member of your family

C   A text message to your sister

D   A letter to the local newspaper

E   An information leaflet about bank charges

F   An article about computer games in a magazine for teenage girls

Activity 2

1   Look at each of the language features below. Are they features of formal language or informal language?

No contractions (e.g. *We will not* we'll)

Abbreviations and SMS language

Easy short words

Complex sentences

Slang

Short, simple sentences

2 a Read the confirmation e-mail on the right that Bob has sent to book a go-karting and meal evening on behalf of his company, Computer ServUS.

b Identify examples of informal language that you think are inappropriate for the audience and purpose.

c Write a more formal version of the e-mail.

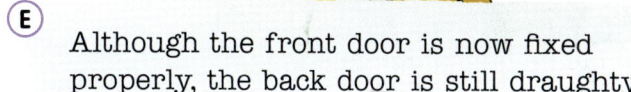
Delete Reply Reply All Forward Print

Just to confirm that I will be turning up with the guys from work next Tuesday (24th June) for the go-karting followed by nosh. As we said the cost will be £15 per person and we will bring this in cash. We'd like a table in the bar. If there is only the restaurant free that's cool. We'll be hitting the town after that so it'd be gr8 if you can sort the cab, as we agreed.

ThanX
Bob ☺

Activity 3

You have recently had a lot of building work carried out at your house. You are extremely unhappy with the builders and need to write a formal letter arguing that they should reduce their price. Look at the following sentences. Choose three that you think would be appropriate in your formal letter and explain why.

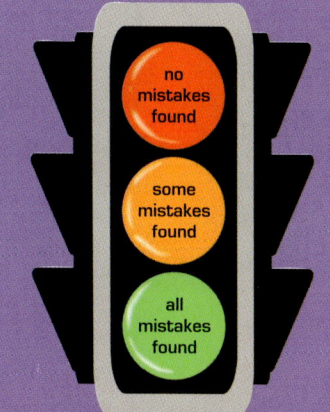

A I am writing to itemise the outstanding issues with the building work.

B The paintwork is scruffy and messy and we're pretty hacked off with the service you've provided.

C There are gaps remaining in the bathroom fixings, despite the visit of your plumber last week.

D The chippy has not been round even though he was booked in last Thursday.

E Although the front door is now fixed properly, the back door is still draughty.

F I would be grateful if you could reply in writing at your earliest convenience.

G Next door's workmanship is head and shoulders better than ours.

Assess your progress

1 Using formal language, write a fifty-word description about a trip you have enjoyed. Add five examples of slang, then work with a partner to read out your formal description. Can they spot the five examples of slang?

2 Assess how well you did, using the traffic lights opposite. Did you spot the deliberate mistakes in your partner's work? Did you manage to include only five examples of slang and no more?

no mistakes found

some mistakes found

all mistakes found

8 Planning a letter

You are learning:
● how to plan and write a formal letter.

Whether you want a new job or a refund on a poor service or product, a formal letter arguing your case can be very effective. Like any piece of writing, a formal letter needs to be carefully planned and correctly laid out.

Activity 1

Can you identify the correct labels for the formal letter below? Write out the correct labels for each number.

(A)  Sender's address

(B)  Signature

(C)  Date

(D) 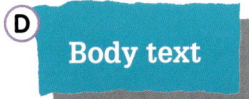 Body text

(E)  Salutation

(F)  Recipient's address

1 **Grove Green** Dental Practice

2 Dental Access Centre
Grove Hospital
Welch Way
Grove
RN34 8RL

3 Mrs A Marsden
42 Millet Way
Grove
RN35 7RL

4 4th March 2008

5 Dear Mrs Marsden

6 Further to your phone call, I enclose the advertisement and application form for the position of Dental Technician at the Dental Access Centre.

I look forward to receiving your application.

7 Yours sincerely

8 *A Pippen*

9 Mrs A Pippen
Human Resources Officer

(G) **Valediction**
- *yours faithfully* when you don't know the name of the recipient
- *yours sincerely* when you know the name of the recipient

(H) **Headed paper when a letter represents a business**

(I) **Sender's name (and job title where appropriate)**

Activity 2

1 Look back at Bob's informal e-mail to the Go Karting Company on page 27. Unfortunately the visit did not go well due to the following issues:
   - the food was cold
   - the 8pm booking was delayed and the go-karting did not start until 8.45. This caused problems for several people who had to leave early
   - the cost of £15 did not include the price of the meal.

2 Write a formal letter of complaint from Bob's boss at Computer ServUS, Sales Manager Eleanor Bright, to complain about the service you received and to ask for a refund. Remember to:
   - use appropriate formal language and layout
   - check your letter for spelling errors
   - include all the relevant points above
   - use your skills of argument.

Sharpen your skills Commas

Commas separate different parts of a sentence. Look at these examples:

Comma because the subordinate clause comes first in the sentence
If your staff had been more polite, the evening would not have been so unpleasant.
    subordinate clause   main clause

No comma because the main clause comes first in the sentence
The evening would not have been so unpleasant if your staff had been more polite.
              main clause   subordinate clause

Commas because of a split main clause
Your staff, who are some of the rudest people I have ever met, did nothing to improve things.
split main clause   subordinate clause   split main clause

Write out the following sentences, putting in commas where they are necessary.
1 Although the food was delayed it was delicious.
2 The quoted meal prices were inaccurate.
3 Many colleagues left the races because of the delays.
4 The event which was quite expensive was a disaster.
5 I was disgusted with the service we received.

Assessment task

Writing: Composition and conventions

Keep our community centre!

The local council is planning to knock down the community centre in your area. This is where the local youth group meets, and it also provides a drop-in centre for teenagers. Other groups in the community, such as toddler groups and the elderly, use the centre too.

The council has produced a poster justifying its actions:

Below are some comments from local people:

> The young people will be out on the streets.

> What do we do for the next three years?

> What about the toddler group and older people? They don't want to meet in the evenings.

YOUR COUNCIL CARES!

Yes, we are knocking down the old community centre – but is that such a loss? The facilities aren't up to modern standards and the building needs urgent repairs.

The new Secondary school, due to be built in the next three years, will include a brand new community room for local people to use. It can be booked through the school and will offer modern facilities for everyone. It will be available in the evenings during term time, and all day during the holidays.

This will provide a much better venue for all community activities.

Your task

Write a letter to the council, arguing that the local community centre should be kept open.

Remember to use:
- a formal, persuasive style, appropriate for a letter to the local council
- paragraphs to organise your ideas
- a range of complex sentences to develop your arguments
- accurate layout for a formal letter.

2 Drama

Objectives

In this unit you will:

Reading

- broaden your reading experience by reading film scripts, TV scripts and plays
- understand and comment on the differences between these types of texts
- comment on how writers' choices and techniques have an effect on readers.

Composition

- plan and write a range of texts, including the opening of a film script and a short scene for a play, using a range of linguistic and literary techniques
- experiment with different ways of presenting texts.

Conventions

- identify and understand the proper use of noun and verb phrases
- understand the use of tense in Standard English and use it in your writing.

Speaking and listening

- choose and evaluate a range of techniques for creating the setting for a play
- work with others to create an improvised performance.

By the end of this unit you will:

- read and answer questions on a playscript (Reading: Understanding the author's craft)
- improvise scenes from a television drama (Speaking and Listening: Drama, role-play and performance)

Cross-curricular links

- **History**
  Cultural, ethnic and religious diversity

1 Playscripts

A playscript is like an instruction book written for directors and actors. It helps them create a performance. A playscript should provide the following information:
● which characters appear in the play
● which characters say which lines
● stage directions describing some of the characters' movements and how they could deliver their lines.

Activity 1

Look at the playscript and novel extract.

1 How are they visually different?

2 What information do you notice at the start of the playscript? How does this immediately tell you what type of text this is?

ACT ONE
Scene One

The action takes place in The Palace – a splendid, if faded, old country house hotel with a grand verandah, a sweeping staircase and stone steps down to fine gardens. As Natalie introduces the story, everyone on stage is silently and unobtrusively reading newspapers, sipping drinks, studying paperwork etc., until suddenly they are galvanised into more bustling life. From time to time, various different guests, crossing the public rooms, waiting on sofas, or dropping keys off at reception, etc., give the impression of a quiet and well-heeled, gradually changing clientele.

NATALIE Meet everyone. That's Mr Scott-Henderson. He practically lives here. I'm not even sure he's got another home. These are Miss Ferguson and Mrs Pettifer. They're practically fixtures as well. I don't know those guests over there. They only checked in this morning. Here is my Dad.

MR BARNES (*on the telephone*) A south-facing double room. Yes indeed. And dinner on both evenings. Thursday and Friday next.

Opening to the playscript of *The Tulip Touch*

Chapter One

You shouldn't tell a story till it's over, and I'm not sure this one is. I'm not even certain when it really began, unless it was the morning Dad thrust my bawling brother Julius back in Mum's arms and picked up the ringing telephone.

'The Palace? Why ever would they want me at the Palace?'

Anyone listening might have begun to think of royal garden parties, or something. But even back then, when I heard people saying things like 'the black horse' or 'the palace', I got a different picture. And that's because I've lived in hotels all my life…

Opening to the novel The Tulip Touch by Anne Fine

Activity 2

Novels are designed to be read by one person at a time. Playscripts are designed to be performed by a group of people, who each take a role.

1   Read the playscript and the opening of the novel *The Tulip Touch*. Using a table like the one below, explore how the same story is told in different ways.

Questions	The playscript of *The Tulip Touch*	The novel of *The Tulip Touch*
a How does each text start?	Opens with a description of a possible backdrop. Instructions are given to the actors: 'everyone is on stage silently'	
b Where is each story set? How is this information provided?		The story is set in the Palace Hotel; we are told this through a telephone conversation
c How are the characters introduced?		
d How is the page laid out?		In sentences and paragraphs

2   Write down three key differences between the openings of the novel and the play. For each one, give an example and write a sentence or two explaining **why** they are different.

Explanation

> **backdrop** a painted scene placed at the back of the stage

Assess your progress

Read your answer to question 2 and use the table below to decide your level of understanding. What could you have included in your explanation to improve your level?

Level 4	Level 5	Level 6
I understand that a novel and a playscript are different and I can name two differences between the two types of writing	I understand how a playscript and novel are different and can give examples of the differences between them	I understand how a playscript and novel are different and can comment on why they are different

2 Dramatic techniques

You are learning:
- to understand the importance of dramatic techniques and their effect on an audience.

Novels and playscripts are often made into films. Have you ever read a book that you thought would make a great film?

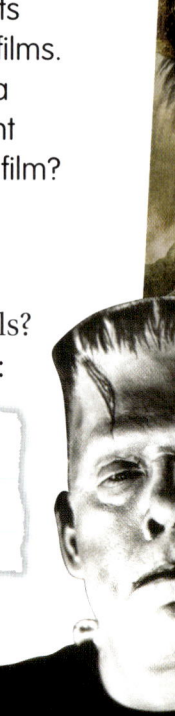

Activity 1

How many films can you think of that were originally novels? Try to include lots of different genres of novel, for example:

- classics: *Frankenstein* by Mary Shelley
- action / adventure: *Stormbreaker* by Anthony Horowitz

Activity 2

1   Read the opening to the novel *Keeper* by Mal Peet.

Paul Faustino slid a blank into the tape recorder and stabbed at a couple of buttons. Then he slapped the machine and said, 'Who is the top football writer in South America? Who is the number one football writer in South America?'

The man looking out of the window didn't turn round. There was a smile in his voice when he said, 'I don't know, Paul. Who?'

'Me. I am. And will the boss buy me a decent tape recorder? No, she will not.' He slapped the machine again and a green light came up on the display. Faustino immediately sat down in front of the small microphone and spoke into it.

'Testing. Date August second. Tape one. Interview: Paul Faustino of *La Nación* talks to the greatest goalkeeper in the history of the world, the man who two days ago took in his hands the World Cup in front of eighty thousand fans and two hundred and twenty million TV viewers.'

He jabbed buttons, rewound the tape and played it back.

Faustino's office was on the seventh floor of a block perched on one of the hills that looked down on the city. The big man standing at the window found it easy enough to imagine himself a hawk coasting over the grid of buildings and the drifting white and red lights of the traffic. Somewhere beyond that carpet of lights and just below the edge of the stars was the forest.

He was tall, exactly six feet four inches, and heavy with it. But when he turned from the window and went to the table where Faustino was sitting, his movements were light and quick and it seemed to the football writer that the big man had somehow glided across the room and into the chair opposite his.

'Are you ready to begin, Gato?' Faustino had his finger on the pause button. On the table between them were a desk lamp that threw hard shadows onto the faces of the two men; also, two bottles of water, a jug filled with ice, Faustino's packet of cigarettes.

And a not very tall chunk of gold. It was in the shape of two figures, wearing what looked like nightdresses, supporting a globe. It was not very beautiful. From where he was sitting, it looked rather like an alien with an oversized bald head. And every footballer in the world wanted it.

The World Cup. It burned in the lamplight.

The big man folded his huge hands together on the tabletop. 'So. Where shall we begin?' he said.

2 Imagine the opening of this novel as a film. Answer these questions to help you:

a Setting
   - Where is the story set?
   - How will you give the audience this information in your film?
   - How would you give this information if you were producing a play?

b Atmosphere
   - The mood or atmosphere of a scene can be created using the characters' actions and dialogue, by the setting, and by music. What type of atmosphere will you create at the start of the film?
   - What will you use to create this atmosphere?

c Character
   - How would you describe the two characters in this scene? Use quotations from the extract to support your answers.
   - Which actors would you cast as these characters?

d Drama
   - How will you gain the audience's attention for the opening of your film?

Activity 3

Transform the opening of *Keeper* into a play script. Look back at the script on page 32 to help you.

Sharpen your skills Phrases

1 A phrase is a group of words built up on a single word. A noun phrase is a group of words that includes a noun (the head or most important word) and other words which add information and description to it. In this example, the noun phrases are underlined and the headwords have been circled:

'The multiplex cinema by the supermarket is showing the best film in the world.'

Identify the noun phrases in the following sentence from *Keeper*.

> 'Paul Faustino of *La Nación* talks to the greatest goalkeeper in the history of the world, the man who two days ago took in his hands the World Cup in front of eighty thousand fans and two hundred and twenty million TV viewers.'

2 The verb in a sentence is called the verb phrase. Sometimes these contain more than one verb: the main verb and one or more auxiliary verbs. They can also include adverbs and prepositions. In the sentence below, the main verbs have been circled, the verb phrase is underlined:

'I quickly decided that I would rush to the cinema.'

   adverb   auxiliary verb   preposition

3 Draw a stick figure of a football player (or any other sports person).

4 Around the stick figure write three sentences describing their abilities.

5 Underline and label the noun and verb phrases.

6 Circle the headwords in the noun phrases and the main verbs in the verb phrases.

3 Settings and openings

You are learning:
- to explore how stage settings can be created and openings can grab an audience's attention.

A story can take its audience anywhere: to every corner of the world, to the edge of the universe. A theatre stage is a small space in which to tell these stories.

Activity 1

1   The setting for a play is suggested by the stage set with painted scenery and props, lighting and sound effects. Using only one prop, plus lighting and sound effects, write a short description of how you could suggest the following settings to an audience:

	One prop	Lighting	Sound effects
A school playground			
A city at night			
A deserted graveyard at night			
A busy beach in summer time			

Activity 2

The stage is set, the curtain goes up and you must grab your audience's attention with your opening scene. Shakespeare is perhaps the most influenial of all playwrights, and he opens many of his plays with very dramatic first scenes.

Romeo and Juliet

Act 1 Scene 1: a huge and bloody sword fight between two feuding families

The Tempest

Act 1 Scene 1: a terrifying storm at sea wrecks the ship on which the characters are sailing

Hamlet

Act 1 Scene 1: the ghost of the recently deceased King is seen walking the battlements of his castle

1   Select one of these opening scenes. Describe which props, lighting and sound effects you could use, explaining your choices.

2   Read this summary of *The Hound of the Baskervilles* by Sir Arthur Conan Doyle. Which of the characters or incidents would you focus on in an opening scene to grab your audience's attention?

> Sir Charles Baskerville is dead. He seems to have fallen victim to the curse of the Baskervilles: a ghostly, ferocious black hound roams the lonely moors of Devon around the old family home, killing any family member who comes to live there. Sir Charles' nephew, Henry, is due to move into the house. A family friend, Dr Mortimer, asks the great detective Sherlock Holmes to solve the mystery and save Henry's life.

3   Design the set for your opening scene to *The Hound of the Baskervilles*. How would you use scenery, props, lighting and sound effects to create the scene and atmosphere for the characters and events you have chosen?

In the opening scene...	Scenery	Props	Lighting	Sound effects

4 Plot

You are learning:
● to identify and explore the plot structure of radio, television and film drama.

The plot is the sequence in which the events of a story take place. No story is entirely original, and most effective and engaging stories follow a pattern.

Activity 1

In 1863, the German writer Freytag devised a diagram explaining how stories are usually structured. It later became known as Freytag's triangle or pyramid.

It divides the action into five stages.

1 **Exposition**: the story is set up, the characters are introduced.
2 **Rising action**: a conflict or problem occurs.
3 **Climax**: the conflict reaches an extreme turning point.
4 **Falling action**: events progress towards an ending.
5 **Denouement** or **resolution**: events are resolved, either happily or tragically.

Climax

Rising action   Falling action

Exposition   Denouement

1 Even short comedy sketches follow the structure of Freytag's triangle. Read this script from *Fawlty Towers*.

The hotel lobby. Things are busy; Mr Thurston approaches Polly. Mrs Richards comes in through the main door, followed by a taxi driver carrying her case.

Polly (*to Thurston*) Oh, hello … can I help you?

Mrs Richards Girl! Would you give me change for this, please.

Polly In one moment – I'm just dealing with this gentleman. Yes, Mr Thurston?

Mrs Richards What?

Thurston Thank you. I was wondering if you could …

Mrs Richards I need change for this.

Polly In a moment – I'm dealing with this gentleman.

Mrs Richards But I have a taxi driver waiting. Surely this gentleman wouldn't mind if you just gave me change.

Polly (*to Thurston*) Do you?

Thurston No, no, go ahead.

Polly (*giving Mrs Richards her change*) There you are.

Thurston Can you tell me how to get to Glendower Street …

Mrs Richards has paid the driver, who exits. She turns back to Polly.

Mrs Richards Now, I've booked a room and bath with a sea view for three nights …

Polly (*to Thurston*) Glendower Street? (*Gets a map.*)

Thurston Yes.

Mrs Richards You haven't finished with me.

Polly Mrs? …

Mrs Richards Mrs Richards. Mrs Alice Richards.

Polly Mrs Richards, Mr Thurston. Mr Thurston, Mrs Richards. (*Mrs Richards, slightly thrown, looks at Mr Thurston.*) Mr Thurston is the gentleman I am attending to at the moment.

Mrs Richards What?

Polly Mr Thurston is the gentleman I am attending to …

Mrs Richards Don't shout, I'm not deaf.

Polly Mr Thurston was here before you, Mrs Richards.

Mrs Richards But you were serving me.

Polly I gave you change, but I hadn't finished dealing with him. (to Thurston) Glendower Street is this one here, just off Chester Street.

Mrs Richards Isn't there anyone else in attendance here? Really, this is the most appalling service I've ever …

Polly (*spotting Manuel*) Good idea! Manuel! Could you lend Mrs Richards your assistance in connection with her reservation. (*to Thurston*) Now… (*She continues to give Thurston directions.*)

Mrs Richards (*to Manuel*) Now, I've reserved a very quiet room, with a bath and a sea view. I specifically asked for a sea view in my written confirmation, so please be sure I have it.

Manuel *Qué?*

Mrs Richards … What?

Manuel …*Qué?*

Mrs Richards K?

Manuel *Si.*

Mrs Richards C? (*Manuel nods.*) KC? (*Manuel looks puzzled.*) KC? What are you trying to say?

Manuel No, no – *Qué?* – what?

Mrs Richards K – what?

Manuel *Si! Qué?* – what?

Mrs Richards C. K. Watt?

Manuel … Yes.

Mrs Richards Who is C. K. Watt?

Manuel *Qué?*

Mrs Richards Is it the manager, Mr Watt?

Manuel Oh manager!

Mrs Richards He *is*.

Manuel Ah … Mr Fawlty.

Mrs Richards What?

Manuel Fawlty.

Mrs Richards What are you talking about, you silly little man. (*Turns to Polly, Mr Thurston having gone.*) What is going on here? I ask him for my room, and he tells me the manager's a Mr Watt and he's aged forty.

Manuel No. No. Fawlty.

Mrs Richards Faulty? What's wrong with him?

Polly It's all right Mrs Richards. He's from Barcelona.

Mrs Richards The manager's from Barcelona?

Manuel No, no. He's from Swanage.

Polly And you're in 22.

Mrs Richards What?

Polly (*leaning over the desk to get close*) You're in room 22. Manuel, take these cases up to 22, will you.

Manuel Si.

He goes upstairs with the cases; Mrs Richards follows.

2 Identify each of the five stages from Freytag's triangle in the script. Remember: some of the stages might be longer or shorter than others.

Activity 2

1 A misunderstanding between characters is one technique used to create comedy. List the different misunderstandings that occur throughout the *Fawlty Towers* script.

2 Plan the plot for a script by drawing a Freytag's triangle that features a misunderstanding. Think carefully about how and where the misunderstanding will need to occur and how it can be created.

3 Write two or three sentences explaining the effect that you think each stage will have on the audience. Would the audience feel excitement, tension, relief, happiness, or something else?

5 Characters

The plot and events in a play or film may interest or excite us, but the characters and their actions are what really grab an audience's attention.

Activity 1

Our Day Out is about a group of students who struggle in school and are being taken on a school trip by their teacher, Mrs Kay. The head teacher suspects that Mrs Kay sees education as 'one long game', so has sent Mr Briggs along to keep an eye on her.

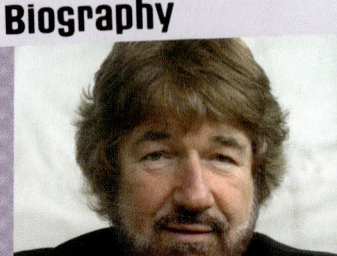

Biography

Willy Russell 1947–
Willy Russell is a famous playwright who grew up in a village outside Liverpool. He qualified as a teacher and taught at Shorefields Comprehensive School from 1973–4. These experiences are what he draws on in his play *Our Day Out.*

1 Read the following extract from *Our Day Out.*

Explanation

> **staccato** short and sharp sounding

At the front of the coach, BRIGGS is climbing aboard. He stands at the front and stares and glares. The KIDS sigh – he is a cloud on the blue horizon.

BRIGGS (suddenly barks) Reilly. Dickson. Sit down!
REILLY Sir, we was only…
BRIGGS (staccato) Sit down, now, come on, move!

(REILLY and DIGGA sit on the two small KIDS who move to make room for them.)

Go on, sort yourselves out!

(He leans across to MRS KAY and speaks quietly.)

You've got some real bright sparks here, Mrs Kay. A right bunch.

2 What do you learn about the characters of Reilly and Digga in this extract? Find a quotation to support each of your points. Think about:
- what they say
- the writer's choice of language suggesting the way they speak
- what they do.

3 Describe Mr Briggs using at least three adjectives. Find a quotation to support each of the adjectives you choose. Think about:
- what he says and his attitude towards the students
- what the stage directions and punctuation suggest about the way he speaks
- what he does.

4 What advice would you give the actors playing the roles of Mr Briggs, Reilly and Digga? Think about how they should speak, move and interact with the other characters.

Activity 2

Write your own short scene between a teacher and a student. Try to use stage directions as well as speech in order to show their character, their relationship and the attitudes that each has. Before you start writing, plan a dramatic ending for your scene.

You could start with one of the ideas on the right, or one of your own.

> **Scenario: A student throws a pencil across the room and the teacher tries to find out who did it.**
> *A pencil flies across the classroom, hitting the window.*
> TEACHER   What was that?
> STUDENT   Nothing, Sir.
> TEACHER   Come on, someone own up, so we can get back to work.

> **Scenario: A teacher is helping a student, when a second student walks in and disrupts the class.**
> TEACHER   So, does that make sense now?
> *The door opens suddenly and hits the wall violently.*

 **Sharpen your skills** **Past tense to present tense**

The following sentences have been written in either the past or present tense.
a   He walked past slowly.
b   The contestants push past, trying to be seen.
c   She stands with an air of dignity around her.
d   The group walks over to where their friends are.
e   The class had not noticed that there was a knock at the door.

1 Identify which sentences are written in the past tense and which ones in the present tense.

2 Change the tense:
- put the sentences in the present tense into the past tense
- put the sentences in the past tense into the present tense.

6 Comedy

You are learning:
● to understand the features of comedy as a genre of drama, using situation comedies as an example.

Sitcom, or situation comedy, is a genre of comedy performance, often produced and shown in a series of episodes. Each episode features the same characters involved in humorous story lines, in a common setting, such as a family home or workplace. Sitcoms were originally devised for radio but today are also found on television.

Situation comedies (sitcoms) are programmes that:
- are meant to make you laugh
- often focus on family life
- are sometimes set in the workplace
- have few sets, which are used over and over again
- tend to be shown during peak viewing times
- are realistic
- appeal to a family audience
- tend to last for half an hour
- are shown at the same time every week
- are easy to understand
- are entertaining
- have canned laughter.

Activity 1

1 Think of as many sitcoms as you can, both American and British. Do they fit all or most of the criteria in the statements above?

2 Using the statements above, write a definition of a sitcom.

Explanation

canned laughter the sound of recorded laughter, played during situation comedies to encourage viewers to laugh

Activity 2

1 *Only Fools and Horses* is a sitcom written by John Sullivan. Read this extract from one of his scripts.

Internal day. Sid's café
Trigger has been awarded a medal and is very proud of his achievement.

Trigger	It's Councillor Murray's idea. She's head of Finance and Facilities at the Town Hall and she says local people should be rewarded for services to the community. A proud moment in my family's history.
Boycie	Trigger, you haven't got a family history. You were created by a chemical spillage at a germ warfare plant somewhere off Deptford High Street.

Trigger	Maybe. But I still feel proud.
Rodney	So what exactly is the medal for?
Trigger	For saving the council money. I happened to mention to her one day that I've had the same broom for the last twenty years. She was very impressed and said 'Have a medal. Twenty years. Long time, Dave.'
Rodney	Yeah, I know, it's two decades innit?
Trigger	I wouldn't go that far, but it's a long time.
	Sid arrives with teas and things.
Del	If you've had that broom for twenty years d'you ever actually sweep the roads with it?
Trigger	Well of course! But I look after it well. We have an old saying that's been handed down to generations of road sweepers: 'Look after your broom …'
Rodney	(*Finishes off saying for him*) And your broom will look after you.
Trigger	… No Dave. It's just 'Look after your broom.'
Rodney	Oh that old saying!
Trigger	Yeah. And that's what I've done. Maintained it for twenty years. This old broom's had seventeen new heads and fourteen new handles in its time.
Sid	Well, how the hell can it be the same broom then?
Trigger	There's the picture of it! What more proof d'you need?
Boycie	Did you tell this to Councillor Murray about the seventeen new heads and fourteen new handles?
Trigger	No. I didn't get technical with her. Anyway I'll see you around.
Sid	Bon appetite.

From 'Heroes and Villains' Christmas Special

2 Why is *Only Fools and Horses* often repeated on television?

3 There are lots of ways to make an audience laugh. Can you identify where the writer has used the following techniques in the extract?

Technique	Definition
Mockery	One character makes fun of another
Irony	Sarcasm, used to imply the opposite of what is actually said
Exaggeration	Making something seem greater or more important than it is
Misunderstanding	The difference between a character's understanding and another character's or the audience's understanding
Stupidity	A character's lack of intelligence

4 Choose one example of a technique you have identified in the extract. Write a sentence or two explaining why you think it is funny.

Assess your progress

How well have you understood the different ways of creating humour?

Level 4	Level 5	Level 6
I can identify where the writer has tried to create humour	I can identify some of the techniques that the writer has used to create humour	I can identify and comment on some of the techniques that the writer has used to create humour

Assessment task
Reading: Understanding the author's craft

Gregory's Girl

Gregory's Girl was originally a film. It is about a boy, Gregory, who wants to do well at football so that he can impress Dorothy, a girl he has fallen for. Dorothy is more interested in football than in Gregory and in the end Gregory finds love elsewhere.

This film has been adapted into a playscript for young people to perform.

Your task

Read the opening of *Gregory's Girl* and complete the questions that follow.

The only permanent set is a full-size football goal.
The play begins at the football match. For the other scenes the setting is minimal, but the posts will be used to support simple backdrops to indicate location.

SCENE 1   The first football match

Our school is playing another school. The opposition is much better organised and more skilful.

(*ANDY is in goal. He prances hopefully. PHIL, the team coach, stands to the left of the posts, in some anguish, MADELINE and RICHARD are amongst the group of spectators to the right of the posts. The reactions range from desperate encouragement to hoots of derision.*)

PHIL   Tackle, will you! Him! For Godsake, tackle him. He's coming inside you. Move. Back. Defence! He's passed it now. Watch the striker. Gregory. GREGORY, watch the striker. ANDY move out. Get off your line, Andy. Now. Dive.

           (*Andy is undecided. A shot rifles past him into the net.*)

           Oh no! Give me strength.

ANDY   (*Retrieves the ball*) I had it covered.

PHIL	Will you stop laughing, Gregory?
ANDY	Misjudged the swerve.
PHIL	Don't waste time. Kick it back. Still time…
ANDY	Reckon the ball's gone out of shape.
PHIL	Get it back to the centre. Still time to go for a draw.
ANDY	That striker's got to be nineteen.
SPECTATOR	Come on, Barry. Show 'em some elbow. What about a professional foul, Barry. Make it worth our while.
PHIL	Eh! None of that.
	(*Whistle. The game restarts.*)
GREGORY	Mark him. MARK HIM!
RICHARD	So why does he play, when he's so bad?
MADELINE	Habit.
RICHARD	I can't see why he can't kick it.
MADELINE	It's complicated. He used to be football mad. Now that he's growing up, you know…'adolescence'.
RICHARD	Oh that.
MADELINE	He wants to impress. Make an impression on the girls. Trouble is he can't play football to save his life.
RICHARD	You said it, Maddy, not me.
MADELINE	Well one doesn't want to be cruel. It's a difficult time.
RICHARD	So they say.
MADELINE	But he's not going to get very far with the girls playing like that.
RICHARD	And looking like that.
MADELINE	I think his proper shorts are in the wash.
PHIL	Take him, Dawson. Take him. You've given him too much space. He'll run round you. Back. All of you BACK. Go left, Andy. Go left. He always shoots left. Shut down the angle. Move. Now!
MADELINE	It's not easy…
RICHARD	He should have been tackled at the half-way line.
MADELINE	…having an adolescent brother.
RICHARD	I see what you mean.
MADELINE	I try to help.

RICHARD   I'm sure he appreciates it, Maddy.

MADELINE   Oh yes, he appreciates it. I just wish he'd listen.

PHIL   Form up. Move yourselves. There's still time. Chuck it, don't carry it. Alvin, place it. You can't waste time. Take the game to them. Get one back. Salvage some morsel of pride…

(*The final whistle blows. The game is over.*)

ANDY   Not as bad as Millsborough Tech, sir.

PHIL   Don't push your luck, lad.

ANDY   Better look on the bright side, wouldn't you say?

PHIL   I would not.

ANDY   (*Beginning to walk off*) Are you coming, sir?

PHIL   No!

ANDY   I'd appreciate a post-mortem on that first one.

PHIL   Just go on in and get changed.

ANDY   No need to be so frosty. We did our best.

PHIL   Go!

(*Andy trots off, not unduly perturbed by this brush-off. Gregory ambles past Phil. He is laughing. Phil throws the ball at Gregory. He drops it.*)

GREGORY   Terrible game, eh?

PHIL   Very bad. Very, very bad.

GREGORY	You've got to laugh.
PHIL	What have you got to laugh at?
GREGORY	Us.
PHIL	It's really that funny, is it?
GREGORY	We're laughable. We're awful. (*Gregory senses a hurt in Phil. He tries to make amends.*) Football is all about entertainment. We give them a good laugh… It's only a game.
PHIL	It's only eight games. Eight games in a row you've lost.
GREGORY	Can't lose them all. You push us really hard, no mercy, lots of discipline, that's what we need. Get tough.
PHIL	We need goals, son, you're not making any goals. That's your job.
GREGORY	Nobody's perfect. It's a tricky time for me. I'm doing a lot of growing, it slows you down. Five inches this year. (*Gregory crouches down so that he's level with Phil, and their faces are very close together.*) Remember last year I was way down here? (*Gregory is still crouching and staring into Phil's face.*) Are you growing a moustache?
PHIL	I want to make some changes.
GREGORY	Good idea. It'll make you look older though.
PHIL	The team. Changes in the team.
GREGORY	You're the boss.
PHIL	I want to try out some other people.
GREGORY	Switch the team around?
PHIL	Take some people out. I was going to take you out.
GREGORY	You don't want to do that.
PHIL	Yes I do.
GREGORY	You don't.
PHIL	I do.
GREGORY	You don't.
PHIL	I might.
GREGORY	Why me?
PHIL	You said yourself you were going through a tricky time. Take a rest.

GREGORY   No…I'm nearly finished growing. Another couple of inches and that'll be me. I'm going to be fine.

(Phil is silent.)

What about Andy? He's hardly started growing yet. He's going to be real trouble.

(Phil is thinking.)

I'll tell him.

PHIL   I'll tell him. You're in goal. For a trial period of three weeks. That's what I'm telling Andy and that's what I'm telling you.

GREGORY   Have you got a jersey my size? Andy's a lot smaller.

PHIL   Don't worry about the jersey. Three weeks in goal for you and them I'm going to decide.

GREGORY   You're the boss. Who's getting my position?

PHIL   I want to find some new people.

(Phil turns abruptly, although somewhat aimlessly, and sprints off.)

GREGORY   *(Calls after him.)* You won't regret this.

(Gregory goes off, engaged in some elaborate fantasy game.)

1 The play starts with a football match.

   a Explain how this could be difficult to show on stage, and how you might achieve it.

   b Why do you think the writer decided to open the play with this scene?

   c Think of two ways in which a director could make the first moments of the play, before anyone speaks, exciting and dramatic for the audience.

2 Annotate Phil's first speech, below, to show his different feelings and how they build up excitement in this opening part of the scene.

> PHIL   Tackle, will you! Him! For Godsake, tackle him. He's coming inside you. Move. Back. Defence! He's passed it now. Watch the striker. Gregory. GREGORY, watch the striker. ANDY move out. Get off your line, Andy. Now. Dive.
>
> (*Andy is undecided. A shot rifles past him into the net.*)
>
> Oh no! Give me strength.

3 What impression do you get of Gregory from this scene?
   You should comment on:
   ● what Phil says about Gregory
   ● what Madeline and Richard say about him
   ● what Gregory himself says.

4 How does Madeline and Richard's choice of language suggest that they are more grown-up than Gregory?

   Support your answer by picking out the words and phrases each of them uses and commenting on them.

5 This play is a comedy.

   What techniques does the writer use in this opening scene that are intended to make the audience laugh? Look at the list of techniques on page 43 to help you.

6 Write the next scene of the play, in which Gregory and Madeline are telling their parents about the football match over dinner.
   You could use these ideas to help you:
   ● Their parents are very keen to hear all about the match
   ● Gregory uses exaggeration to make his efforts sound more impressive
   ● Madeline is reluctant to talk about the game.

7 Improvising a scene

Improvisation means a piece of non-scripted dramatic work that you have made up yourself. The following activities will encourage you to think on your feet as well as improving your listening and concentration skills.

Activity 1

Imagine that you are one of the characters from the list below. Write down a list of questions that you can answer in role as the character.

- a spoilt child who is trying to get their own way
- a soldier in the British armed forces who is keen to obey
- a famous actor who is bored with answering questions
- an argumentative politician
- a talkative comedian.

Activity 2

1 Read the following guidelines for improvising. The examples are taken from an improvised scene called 'A major incident in the classroom'.

Do	A good example	Don't	A bad example
Plan your characters' attitudes to the situation: conflicting attitudes create drama	Have one character with one attitude and the other with the opposite attitude, e.g. angry and relaxed	Just think about the events in your improvisation	If everyone is angry, the shouting and fighting will get boring for the audience
Enter or exit with a purpose: an action, emotion or attitude	'Sorry I'm late Miss, but my budgie died this morning. (*sniff*)'	Wander in and hope for the best	'Er...hello.'
Start halfway through the action	'Miss, Miss, Barry's stolen my best pencil!'	Start with the characters introducing each other	'Good morning, children, my name is Miss Brown and I am your new teacher.'
Build on your partner's improvisation	'Oh Barry, this is the fifth time I've had to speak to you this lesson...'	Deny or disagree with your partner's improvisation	'No you're not, you're the school caretaker.'
Give lots of detail for your partner to respond to	'...and you've already had three detentions this week!'	Say things to which there are few possible replies	'Stop it, Barry!'

2 You are going to carry out your own improvisation. The following are possible ideas that have been adapted from the texts included in this unit. You could use one of these ideas for your improvisation.

● school trips
● growing up and not being very good at a particular activity
● unexpected events on public transport
● a group of friends teasing each other.

a Choose one of these ideas – or come up with one of your own.
b Use the table on page 50 to help you decide on the different characters you will have in your improvisation.

Activity 3

Use this flowchart to develop your character. It will help you think of what to say and how to react to what the other actors say. For every question you answer from the flowchart, ask another question from the question bank – and answer it.

Question bank
Why?
What about?
What for?
How does s/he feel about that?
Who does that?
How?
Will that always be true?

1 Choose an emotion that will sum up your character in one word. Are they happy, angry, sad, bored, worried, frightened…?

2 What is your character's job?

3 What has happened to your character so far today? Write three or four sentences from their diary for today. Try to think of dramatic or interesting events.

Worried.
Why? Because she has lied to her mum.
What about? Where she's going tonight.

Student.
How does she feel about that?
She likes school when she does well but sometimes gets annoyed when she doesn't.

Woke up and had an argument with her mum. Left home late and was late for school. Got told off.
How does she feel about that? Annoyed.

Amy

8 What is your character's name?

Letitia.
Why? They live on the same street and have been in the same class since Year 1.
Will that always be true? No. Letitia is starting to annoy her.

7 Who is your character's best friend? Describe them.

4 What is your character wearing? Describe their clothes. Now add some more adjectives to develop the description.

School uniform. Scruffy. Muddy.
Why? She can't find her clean uniform because her room is a mess.

5 Describe your character's home.

Lives with mum, baby sister and hamster. Mum spends all her time and energy on baby sister.
How does she feel about that? A bit jealous and annoyed sometimes.

6 Describe your character's family.

A small house, kept neat, clean, tidy.
Who does that? Mum works hard all day and then cleans up, which can make her angry.

Activity 4

1   Now that you have developed your characters, use the table on page 50 to think about:
    - how you will start your improvisation
    - how your improvisation might develop.

2   Perform your improvisation.

3   State two positive things about your performance and one thing that you would like to improve. You will work towards meeting this target during the next activity.

Assess your progress

Below are the Speaking and Listening levels. What level do you think your performance was and why?

Level 4	Level 5	Level 6
• I talked and listened with some confidence • The language I used was appropriate for our performance • I listened carefully to others and responded to what they said	• I talked and listened confidently • I adapted my choice of language to suit our performance • I am beginning to vary my expression and the words I use • I added my ideas to the improvisation, which shows that I listened carefully to what other people said	• I talked and listened very confidently • I confidently adapted my talk to suit our performance • I am good at varying my expression and vocabulary • I developed our improvisation with my own ideas and by listening to and building on others' ideas

Sharpen your skills Future tense

There are two ways of putting a verb into the future tense: by adding 'will' or 'going to' into the verb phrase. For example:

Past tense	Present tense	Future tense
I worked hard on my homework.	I work hard on my homework.	I will work hard on my homework.
I ate a sandwich.	I am eating a sandwich.	I am going to eat a sandwich.

Using the future tense, write down two Speaking and Listening targets that you will achieve and say how you will achieve them.
- I will…
- To achieve this I am going to…

Assessment task

Speaking and Listening: Drama, role-play and performance

Where have you been?

Below is the opening of a scene from a television drama. It is about a teenager called David, his sister Jo, and his parents, Diane and Stuart. At the beginning of the scene, David has not returned home in time for dinner.

Diane: Where is he? He knows it's dinner time...

Stuart: He should have phoned but I expect he forgot. Come on, love, let's eat. I'm starving. He'll be back soon...

Diane: I can't relax when I don't know where he is. Why can't he just ring and let us know where he is? His dinner will get cold.

Jo: He'll be back soon, Mum.

Diane: He'd better be...

(*The door opens and in comes David wearing a hoodie with the hood up and gloves.*)

Diane: Oh, David...

Stuart: There you are, son, we were just wondering where you'd got to. Now come in and have some dinner.

Diane: Where have you been and what have you been up to? Why are you wearing that hood and those gloves?

David: Oh forget it, Mum. What's for dinner?

Your task

Use this scene as the starting point for **two** improvised scenes from a television drama.

In each scene you should:
- develop the characters in different ways
- explore a different idea or create a different mood or atmosphere.

For example, you could focus on relationships between parents and teenagers and the lack of communication between them; you could make it a comedy or a mystery. You don't need to provide an 'ending'; you could end on a cliffhanger or at any point you like. You are only developing part of the whole drama.

You need to remember to:
- develop each character convincingly in two different ways using voice, mannerisms, gestures and movements
- show how the relationships develop differently in each scene
- create a particular mood or atmosphere for the audience in each case.

8 Directing a scene

You are learning:
● to make decisions about how you would direct a scene and make notes about the playscript for the actors.

A good script is only the first step towards a performance. To engage and entertain an audience, the director and the actors must decide how they will perform and deliver the script.

Activity 1

1 Facial expressions tell an audience a lot about how a character is feeling and what they are thinking. What do these facial expressions suggest to you?

2 Read this short drama extract.

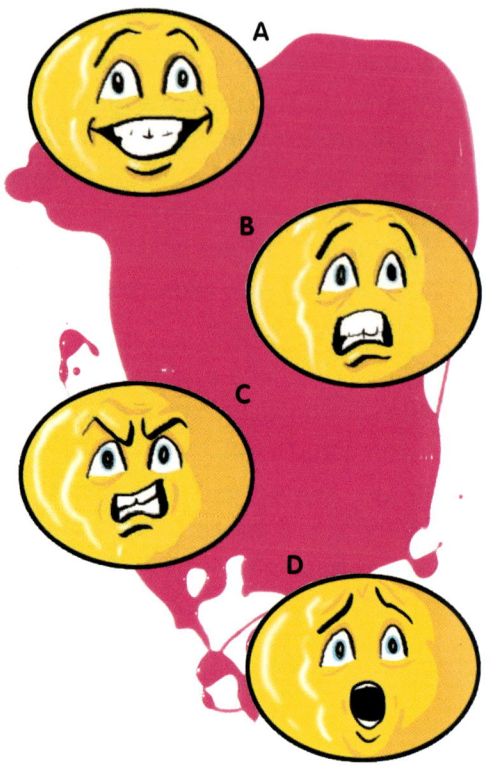

> Alan: I can't believe it.
> Jane: What's happened?
> Alan: They said this would never happen and it has.
> Jane: What is it? What is it?
> Alan: I told them it would, but they didn't believe me.
> Jane: And you were right?
> Alan: I usually am.

3 What do you think has happened? How are these characters feeling?

4 Draw a face for each line of the script, showing the expression you think the actor should use. Try to use as many different emotions as possible.

Activity 2

1 Look at this diagram of an actor. How would you describe his feelings?

2 Draw a diagram for each of the character's lines in the extract above, showing how the actors should use body language to support their facial expressions.

3 What other advice would you give the actors performing this scene? Think about tone of voice and pace (the speed at which they deliver their lines and any pauses).

Activity 3

Read the extract from *Henry IV Part One* Act One Scene 2, both Shakespeare's original and the modern version.

At the start of the play, Prince Henry is rebelling against his father, the King, and spends a great deal of time bantering with his friend, Falstaff.

SCENE II. London. An apartment of the Prince's.
Enter the PRINCE OF WALES and FALSTAFF

FALSTAFF

Now, Hal, what time of day is it, lad?

PRINCE HENRY

Thou art so fat-witted, with drinking of old sack and unbuttoning thee after supper and sleeping upon benches after noon, that thou hast forgotten to demand that truly which thou wouldst truly know. What a devil hast thou to do with the time of the day? Unless hours were cups of sack and minutes capons and clocks the tongues of bawds and dials the signs of leaping-houses and the blessed sun himself a fair hot wench in flame-coloured taffeta, I see no reason why thou shouldst be so superfluous to demand the time of the day.

FALSTAFF

Indeed, you come near me now, Hal; for we that take purses go by the moon and the seven stars, and not by Phoebus, he, 'that wandering knight so fair'. And, I prithee, sweet wag, when thou art king, as, God save thy grace, – majesty I should say, for grace thou wilt have none, –

PRINCE HENRY

What, none?

FALSTAFF

No, by my troth, not so much as will serve to prologue to an egg and butter.

SCENE II. London. An apartment of the Prince's.
Enter the PRINCE OF WALES and FALSTAFF

FALSTAFF
Now, Hal, what time is it, boy?

PRINCE HENRY
You are so fat-headed from drinking booze and loosening your trousers after dinner and sleeping on benches in the afternoon, you have forgotten how to ask what you want to know. Why do you need to know what time it is? Unless hours were cups of wine and minutes were chickens, clocks were whores' tongues, sundials were whorehouse signs, and the sun a hot woman in a flame-coloured dress, I can't see why you would need to know the time.

FALSTAFF
You're near the truth now, Hal, for we thieves work at night, by the moon and stars, not by the sun. And I beg you, pretty boy, when you are king, God save Your Grace – or perhaps I should say Your Majesty as you don't have any grace –

PRINCE HENRY
What, none at all?

FALSTAFF
No, not even enough to say grace before you eat an egg and butter.

Explanation

Grace Falstaff makes a pun on two meanings of this word:
1 a short prayer before a meal
2 elegance, beauty, kindness

1 From Shakespeare's original, answer the following questions:
   a Falstaff criticises Prince Henry in the extract. What does he say about him?
   b Write down the five different ways in which Falstaff addresses Prince Henry in this extract.
   c What does this suggest about the relationship between them?

2 From the modern version, answer the following questions:
   a Write down three ways in which Prince Henry describes Falstaff.
   b What do they suggest about the relationship between them?

Using both versions, answer the following questions:

3 How can you tell that these two characters are not annoyed or insulted by the rude things they say about each other?

4 Prince Henry's father is King Henry IV of England. Prince Henry is the heir to his throne. How could you show that he has a much higher status than Falstaff?

5 Make a list of all the stage directions you can – and where you would put them in the script – to show how Falstaff and Prince Henry are teasing each other. Think about:
   ● facial expressions
   ● body language, movement or actions
   ● tone of voice
   ● pace.

   Here are some to get you started:
   ● Falstaff taps Hal on the shoulder
   ● Hal grimaces at Falstaff
   ● Hal's voice becomes higher and higher, as he exaggerates more and more.

6 Check that you have used at least one stage direction of each type in the list in question 5.

7 Act out the scene, using all of your stage directions.

3 Detective stories

Objectives

In this unit you will:

Reading

- read between the lines, inferring meaning to solve detective mysteries
- follow the way that writers develop ideas and themes in texts
- make precise points about texts you read and provide evidence to support them.

Writing

- explore, problem-solve, connect and shape ideas, choosing the best way to plan your writing
- explore techniques used by writers to develop your own fiction writing
- choose from a range of language techniques to create a specific effect.

Conventions

- develop your use of grammatical conventions.

By the end of this unit you will:

- identify and compare the elements of a detective story in two different examples (Reading: Understanding the author's craft)
- write the opening for a detective story (Writing: Composition and conventions).

Cross-curricular links

- **History**
  Using evidence
- **Citizenship**
  Critical thinking and enquiry

1 Features of the detective genre

You are learning:
- to identify the key features of the detective genre.

In 1841, Edgar Allan Poe wrote what many people think is the first detective story: *The Murders in the Rue Morgue*. It tells the tale of a double murder in a room locked from the inside, and how amateur detective C. Auguste Dupin solves the crime with his powers of deduction and observation. Readers were instantly hooked, and they have been reading detective fiction ever since.

Activity 1

Fictional detectives are some of the most popular and well-known characters in books and films. Which of the detectives listed below have you seen or read or heard of? What do you know about them? Where are they from? Do any of them have a catchphrase that you can remember?

Explanation

deduction working something out from the clues

Sherlock Holmes	Miss Marple
The Famous Five	Hercule Poirot
Inspector Morse	You – if you've ever played
Columbo	the board game, Cluedo

Use a table like the one below to write down anything you can remember:

Name of detective	What I know about them
Sherlock Holmes	Lived on Baker Street
Miss Marple	

Activity 2

Read these true stories. Can you work out who committed the crime? The solution is at the bottom of page 59.

B

Murder 2
Alice Smith died on 12th December 1913. She and her husband, Charles Smith, were staying at a boarding house in Blackpool, owned by Mr and Mrs Crossley. She had gone to take a bath and never returned. Mr Crossley remembered that, when her body was found, her head was at the foot of the bath. The inquest concluded that Alice had 'accidentally drowned through heart failure when in the bath'. Her husband received the £500 for which Alice's life had been insured.

A

Murder 1
Bessie Williams was found dead in the bath at 80 High Street, Herne Bay, on 13th July 1912. It was discovered that only five days earlier she had made a will leaving everything – 2,579 pounds, 13 shillings and 7 pence – to her husband, Henry Williams. Dr Frank French examined Bessie's body, and declared that she had had an epileptic fit and drowned. He said: 'I have no reason to suspect any other cause than drowning.' The jury returned a verdict of 'Death by misadventure'.

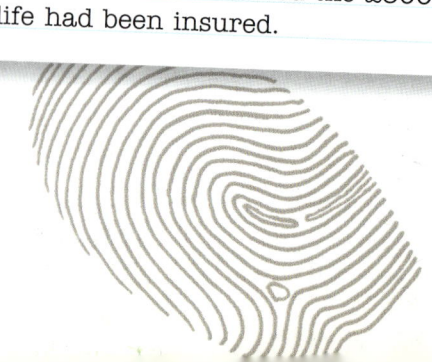

C

Murder 3

Margaret Elizabeth Lloyd and her husband, John Lloyd, were staying at a boarding house at 14 Bismark Road, in Highgate, London. On the afternoon of 18th December 1914, Margaret Lloyd had visited her solicitor in Islington and made a will leaving everything to her husband. That evening, Mr Lloyd told the owner of the house that he was going out to buy some tomatoes while his wife had a bath. When he returned he called to his wife but she did not reply. He entered the bathroom and found her dead in the bath. The inquest of 1st January 1915 returned a verdict of accidental death.

Activity 3

1 Think about your investigation of the mystery of the Brides in the Bath. Did this story capture your imagination? Why? What are the ingredients for a good detective story?

   a Copy and add to the list below.

   > **A recipe for a successful detective story**
   > • A clever criminal
   > • Some clues

   b Explain the importance of the features you have chosen.

   > This is an important ingredient in detective stories because …

2 Look at your recipe for a successful detective story:

   a Which ingredients should come near the beginning of the story?

   b Which ingredients should come in the middle?

   c Which ingredients should come near the end?

3 Why do you think detective stories are structured in this way?

The Solution

In January 1915, Detective Inspector Neil received a letter from Mr Crossley of Blackpool containing two newspaper cuttings about the deaths of Margaret Lloyd and Alice Smith. Mr Crossley suggested there was a connection and the police should investigate. It was found that George Joseph Smith had been married five times, each time under a different name. On 23rd March 1915, he was charged with the murders of Bessie Williams, Alice Smith, and Margaret Lloyd. He was hanged at Maidstone Gaol on 13th August 1915.

Assess your progress

This table shows you how to get better at the key reading skills used on these two pages. How well are you doing?

Level 4	Level 5	Level 6
I understand how the ingredients for a detective story are structured	I understand the structure of detective stories and why they are organised in this way	I can comment on the structure of detective stories and the effect the writer wants to achieve

2 Solving a mystery

You are learning:
- to read between the lines of a murder mystery and investigate the rules of detective fiction.

We all like a secret, a mystery, a puzzle. Whether it's a game of Sudoku, a crossword, or *Where's Wally*, we love a mystery, and we love trying to solve it.

Activity 1

1 Read the following text. It's called 'Split Personality', by Mark Turner, and it is one of the shortest crime stories in the world.

He was gorgeous. She was thrilled. But puzzled.

'Why were your other relationships so short?' she wondered aloud as they walked.

He glanced upwards.

'Well, I have this slight problem...'

Later, the detective grimaced at the ghastly sight of the young girl, bloody beneath the full moon.

In the distance, a wolf howled.

2 How many characters are there in this story?

3 What happened in 'Split Personality'? Write a summary of the story in two or three sentences.

4 What ingredients of a detective story can you identify in 'Split Personality'?

Activity 2

1 In 1928, the novelist S.S. Van Dine wrote an article called 'Twenty rules for writing detective stories'. Read this extract from it:

Explanations

> **culprit** the criminal
> **prominent** major or leading

The detective story is a sporting event. And for the writing of detective stories there are very definite rules.

- 🔍 The reader must have equal opportunity with the detective for solving the mystery.
- 🔍 The detective should never turn out to be the culprit.
- 🔍 The culprit must be discovered by logical deduction, not by accident or coincidence.
- 🔍 The detective novel must have a detective in it. His function is to gather clues that will eventually lead to the person who did the dirty work in the first chapter.
- 🔍 There must be a corpse in a detective novel, and the deader the corpse the better. No lesser crime than murder will do.
- 🔍 The culprit must turn out to be someone who has played a prominent part in the story, that is, a person with whom the reader is familiar.
- 🔍 There must be just one culprit, no matter how many murders are committed.
- 🔍 The truth of the problem must at all times be apparent, provided the reader is clever enough to see it. So the reader, if he had been as clever as the detective, could have solved the mystery himself without going on to the final chapter.
- 🔍 A detective novel should contain no long descriptive passages.
- 🔍 A crime in a detective story must never turn out to be an accident.

2 What do you think Van Dine meant when he wrote that a detective story is 'a sporting event'?

3 **a** Which of these rules does the story *Split Personality* stick to?
   b Which rules does it break?

4 How could the story be continued so that it sticks to Van Dine's rules? Write a plan to show your ideas.

Sharpen your skills Modal verbs

Read the following sentences:

I eat more vegetables.
I <u>should</u> eat more vegetables.
I <u>would</u> eat more vegetables.
I <u>could</u> eat more vegetables.
I <u>must</u> eat more vegetables.
I <u>may</u> eat more vegetables.

I <u>might</u> eat more vegetables.
I <u>ought to</u> eat more vegetables.
I <u>can</u> eat more vegetables.
I <u>shall</u> eat more vegetables.
I <u>will</u> eat more vegetables.

In each one, the modal verb has been underlined. What is a modal verb? What difference does the choice of modal verb make to the meaning of the sentence? Which is the strongest modal verb and which is the weakest?

3 Character

You are learning:
- to investigate the character of the detective.

Detective fiction follows the solving of a crime, so we usually see the story through the eyes of the detective. This means that the writer has to make the detective's character interesting and appealing to the reader.

Activity 1

In 1887, Arthur Conan Doyle published *A Study in Scarlet,* introducing readers to the character of Sherlock Holmes. The stories, told by Holmes' friend Dr Watson, were an instant success. In this extract from *A Study in Scarlet,* Dr Watson meets Sherlock Holmes for the first time.

1   Read the extract.

This was a lofty chamber, lined and littered with countless bottles. Broad, low tables were scattered about, which bristled with retorts, test-tubes, and little Bunsen lamps, with their blue flickering flames. There was only one student in the room, who was bending over a distant table absorbed in his work. At the sound of our steps he glanced round and sprang to his feet with a cry of pleasure. 'I've found it! I've found it,' he shouted to my companion, running towards us with a test-tube in his hand. 'I have found a re-agent which is precipitated by haemoglobin, and by nothing else.' Had he discovered a gold mine, greater delight could not have shone upon his features.

'Dr Watson, Mr Sherlock Holmes,' said Stamford, introducing us.

'How are you?' he said cordially, gripping my hand with a strength for which I should hardly have given him credit. 'You have been in Afghanistan, I perceive.'

'How on earth did you know that?' I asked in astonishment.

'Never mind,' said he, chuckling to himself. 'The question now is about haemoglobin. No doubt you see the significance of this discovery of mine?'

'It is interesting, chemically, no doubt,' I answered, 'but practically...'

'Why, man, it is the most practical medico-legal discovery for years. Don't you see that it gives us an infallible test for blood stains. Come over here now!' He seized me by the coat-sleeve in his eagerness, and drew me over to the table at which he had been working. 'Let us have some fresh blood,' he said, digging a long

Biography

Arthur Conan Doyle (1859–1930) was a Scottish-born author famous for his stories about the detective Sherlock Holmes, who never failed to solve a crime, however complicated.

Explanations

haemoglobin the protein in red blood cells that carries oxygen
infallible foolproof, cannot fail
precipitate (in chemistry) solid that appears when two solutions are mixed together
retort a flask used in chemical experiments

bodkin into his finger, and drawing off the resulting drop of blood in a chemical pipette. 'Now, I add this small quantity of blood to a litre of water. You perceive that the resulting mixture has the appearance of pure water. The proportion of blood cannot be more than one in a million. I have no doubt, however, that we shall be able to obtain the characteristic reaction.' As he spoke, he threw into the vessel a few white crystals, and then added some drops of a transparent fluid. In an instant the contents assumed a dull mahogany colour, and a brownish dust was precipitated to the bottom of the glass jar.

'Ha! ha!' he cried, clapping his hands, and looking as delighted as a child with a new toy. 'What do you think of that?'

'It seems to be a very delicate test,' I remarked.

'Beautiful! Beautiful! The old Guiacum test was very clumsy and uncertain. So is the microscopic examination for blood corpuscles. The latter is valueless if the stains are a few hours old. Now, this appears to act as well whether the blood is old or new. Had this test been invented, there are hundreds of men now walking the earth who would long ago have paid the penalty of their crimes.'

'Indeed!' I murmured.

2   What does this extract tell you about the character of Sherlock Holmes? Use a table like the one below to record your findings. Choose a quotation to support each of your deductions.

	Quotation	What this tells us	What the writer's choice of language suggests
The setting in which we see Holmes	'tables were scattered about, which bristled with retorts, test-tubes, and little Bunsen lamps'	Holmes is a scientist, perhaps disorganised but very involved in his work	'scattered' suggests it is chaotic. 'bristled' suggests it is crowded.
What Holmes does			
What Holmes says			
The language Holmes uses			
Holmes' attitude to his experiments			
Holmes' attitude to criminals			

3   What does the extract **not** tell us about Sherlock Holmes?

4   Based on your investigation of the text, think of five words or phrases to describe Sherlock Holmes.

Activity 2

Miss Marple, a character created by Agatha Christie, is an elderly lady who investigates and solves the most puzzling murders far more quickly than the police. This is how Christie introduces her in the novel, *A Pocketful of Rye*.

1   Read the extract.

An elderly lady travelling by train had bought three morning papers, and each of them as she finished it, she folded it and laid it aside, showed the same headline. It was no longer a question now of a small paragraph hidden away in the corner of the papers. There were headlines with flaring announcements of Triple Tragedy at Yewtree Lodge.

The old lady sat very upright, looking out of the window of the train, her lips pursed together, an expression of distress and disapproval on her pink and white wrinkled face. Miss Marple had left St Mary Mead by the early train, changing at the junction and going on to London terminus and thence on to Baydon Heath.

At the station she signalled a taxi and asked to be taken to Yewtree Lodge. So charming, so innocent, such a fluffy and pink and white old lady was Miss Marple that she gained admittance to what was now practically a fortress in a state of siege far more easily than could have been believed possible. Though an army of reporters and photographers were being kept at bay by the police, Miss Marple was allowed to drive in without question, so impossible would it have been to believe that she was anyone but an elderly relative of the family.

2   What does this extract tell you about the character of Miss Marple? Use a table like the one below to record your findings. Choose a quotation to support your deductions.

	Quotation	What this tells us	What the writer's choice of language suggests
Marple's appearance	'lips pursed together, an expression of distress and disapproval on her pink and white wrinkled face'	Elderly, shocked and deeply affected by murder	
How Marple behaves			
Marple's attitude to crime			
Other people's attitudes to Marple			
The adjectives used to describe Marple			

3   What does this extract **not** tell us about Miss Marple?

4   Based on your investigation of the text, think of five words or phrases to describe Miss Marple.

Activity 3

1 Use the flow chart below to design your own character: a new detective who will grab your reader's attention from the first time they are introduced.

A Is your detective male or female?

B Are they a professional detective – is it their only job?

Or an amateur with another job?

What is their other job?

C

What does their office look like?

D What does their house look like?

F What is their attitude to crime and criminals?

Where will they be when you introduce them to the reader?

What will they be doing?

Why are they there?

E How old are they?

What do they look like?

What kind of clothes do they wear?

How do they act or behave?

What kind of language do they use?

2 Choose **three** things to describe when you first introduce your detective to the reader.

3 Agatha Christie **tells** us what Miss Marple is like. For example, she tells us that Marple is 'charming' and 'innocent'. Conan Doyle, however, **shows** us what Holmes is like. For example, he does not **tell** us that Holmes is very dedicated and enthusiastic; he shows us Holmes running towards Watson, shouting excitedly about his discovery.

   a Write a short description of your detective in which, like Agatha Christie, you **tell** the reader what he or she is like.

   b Write a short description of your detective in which, like Conan Doyle, you **show** the reader what he or she is like.

   c Which descriptive method do you prefer? Give a reason for your answer.

Assess your progress

1 Think of three words or phrases to describe your detective. For each word or phrase, find a quotation from the description you wrote in question 3 that shows this is a good way to describe them.

2 Swap your descriptions with a partner. Ask them to write down three words to describe your detective and find quotations to support them.

3 Compare your words. Did you agree with each other? Have you given your reader a good idea of your detective's character?

4 Creating tension

Tension is a key ingredient in crime fiction. It is often built through the situations in which the writer places the characters, and the dialogue they are given.

Activity 1

1   Read the opening paragraphs of *Shatter Proof*, a short story by Jack Ritchie, thinking about how the writer builds tension.

He was a soft-faced man wearing rimless glasses, but he handled the automatic with unmistakable competence.

I was rather surprised at my calmness when I learned the reason for his presence. 'It's a pity to die in ignorance,' I said. 'Who hired you to kill me?'

His voice was mild. 'I could be an enemy in my own right.'

I had been making a drink in my study when I had heard him and turned. Now I finished pouring from the decanter. 'I know the enemies I've made and you are a stranger. Was it my wife?'

He smiled. 'Quite correct. Her motive must be obvious.'

'Yes,' I said. 'I have money and apparently she wants it. All of it.'

He regarded me objectively. 'Your age is?'

'Fifty-three.'

'And your wife is?'

'Twenty-two.'

He clicked his tongue. 'You were foolish to expect anything permanent, Mr Williams.'

I sipped the whiskey. 'I expected a divorce after a year or two and a painful settlement. But not death.'

'Your wife is a beautiful woman, but greedy, Mr Williams. I'm surprised that you never noticed.'

My eyes went to the gun. 'I assume you have killed before?'

'Yes'

'And obviously you enjoy it.'

He nodded. 'A morbid pleasure, I admit. But I do.'

I watched him and waited. Finally I said, 'you have been here more than two minutes and I am still alive.'

'There is no hurry, Mr Williams,' he said softly.

'Ah, then the actual killing is not your greatest joy. You must savour the preceding moments.'

'You have insight, Mr Williams.'

'And as long as I keep you entertained, in one manner or another, I remain alive?'

'Within a time limit, of course.'

Activity 2

There are three things a writer has to think about when creating tension: action, description and dialogue.

1   To what extent does the writer use action to build tension in this extract?

2   Look at the way Ritchie describes the character of the gunman.
   a   Re-read the first five paragraphs. Write down every detail we are told about the gunman. What impression is the writer aiming to give us of this character?
   b   How does the way this character is described help build the tension in this extract?

3   Now look at the way Ritchie has used dialogue in this opening.

   a   Re-read the last ten paragraphs of the extract, from 'My eyes went to the gun'. What do you notice about the length of these paragraphs?
   b   Which details in this dialogue contribute most to building tension? Write a sentence or two explaining your answers.
   c   These ten paragraphs contain 101 words. How many of them are not dialogue?
   d   Why do you think the writer has chosen to concentrate on what the characters say rather than what they do?
   e   Look again at the final paragraph. How does this add to the build-up of tension?

Activity 3

Imagine the detective character you designed in Activity 3 on page 65 meeting a ruthless criminal face to face. Write a short description of what happens.

Remember to:
• plan your paragraphs so they describe one key event
• plan an ending to break or add to the tension
• use short sentences to build tension
• use dramatic vocabulary
• describe how your characters look to show the reader how they are feeling.

Sharpen your skills   Full stops and capital letters

Read the following passage; it has had all the full stops and capital letters removed.

Copy out the passage, inserting the full stops and capital letters where necessary to ensure it makes clear sense.

sherlock holmes and his assistant, dr watson, live in london because of holmes' great intelligence he is very successful at the start of his career he meets watson by accident they decide to share a flat although watson is not as clever as holmes he is very helpful to the great detective solving crime is a hobby, a job, a challenge and a pleasure

5 Plot

You are learning:
● to understand how a writer plots an effective detective story.

The plot of a detective story is usually linear; it follows a line through three stages:

The characters are introduced and a crime takes place

The detective investigates the clues

The crime is solved

Activity 1

This is a summary of Agatha Christie's *A Murder Is Announced*.

Read the summary and answer the questions. It begins with the first stage of the plot:

> 'A murder is announced and will take place on Friday, October 29th, at Little Paddocks, at 6.30 p.m. Friends accept this, the only intimation.'

The set-up:
Letitia Blacklock lives at Little Paddocks in the village of Chipping Cleghorn with:
- her schoolfriend, Dora 'Bunny' Bunner
- Philippa Haymes, a widow who rents a room
- some visiting friends, and brother and sister Patrick and Julia Simmons.

They are all astonished when an advert appears in the local paper.

The crime:
That night, people gather at Little Paddocks. At 6.30, the lights go out, a door opens, a man with a torch shouts 'Stick 'em up!' There are shots: the gunman is dead, and Letitia is bleeding, grazed by a bullet. Miss Marple is called in to investigate.

The dead man:
Rudi Schertz worked at a local hotel. He was overheard trying to borrow money from Letitia. He was paid anonymously to stage a robbery at Little Paddocks, thinking it was a joke.

1

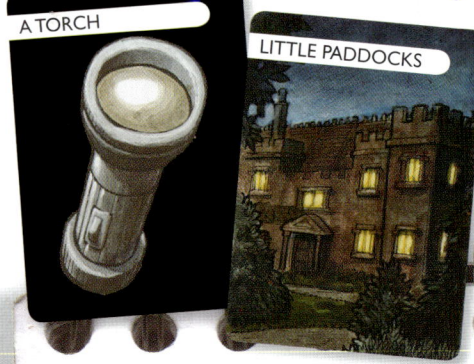

Some background facts:
Letitia worked for a wealthy businessman in Switzerland, Randall Goedler. He died and left his money to his wife; when she dies all the money goes to Letitia. If Letitia dies, it goes to Goedler's nieces, Pip and Emma – but nobody knows who or where they are.
Letitia had a sister, Charlotte, who was born with a goitre, a disfigurement of the neck. Charlotte had surgery to rectify it but died soon after and Letitia came back to England.

More background is discovered:
Julia Simmons reveals she is Emma, Randall Goedler's niece. Patrick is her boyfriend; they pretended to be brother and sister. Philippa Haymes reveals she is Pip, the other niece. Both claim to be innocent.

2

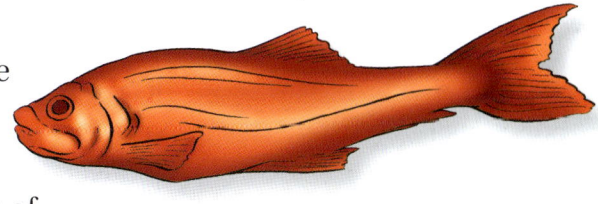

1. How does Christie make us think that many of the characters have a motive for murder?

2. If there is only one murderer, most of these clues must be red herrings (false clues put in by the writer to mislead the reader). Why do detective fiction writers do this?

Having set up the plot, Christie moves into the second stage of her story: introducing more clues – and more murders. Read on.

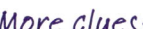

DORA BUNNER

More clues:

Bunny tells Miss Marple that there are two doors into the room where the murder took place; and that a lamp has disappeared from the room. Letitia organises a birthday party for Bunny but Bunny goes to bed early with a headache. She can't find her aspirin so borrows Letitia's. Bunny is found dead the next morning – poisoned.

A BOTTLE OF ASPIRIN

3

A ROPE

More murder!

Miss Hinchcliff and Miss Murgatroyd were at Little Paddocks on the night of the murder. They realise that Miss Murgatroyd was behind the door and could see who was in the room by the light of Rudi's torch. If she can remember who was missing, then she can identify the murderer! She remembers – but is throttled before she can tell anyone.

4

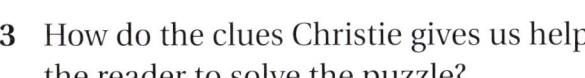

3. How do the clues Christie gives us help the reader to solve the puzzle?

4. Who do you think killed Rudi Scherz? How did you work it out?

Now explore the third and final stage of the plot: the resolution.

The final clue:

Miss Marple is at Little Paddocks one night. She knocks over a glass of water. The lights go out. It seems that a nearby lamp's lead was frayed, and the water blew the fuse.

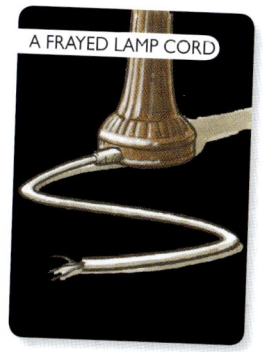

A FRAYED LAMP CORD

5

Miss Marple explains everything

Charlotte did not die – Letitia did. Charlotte posed as Letitia to get her inheritance. She recognised Rudi Scherz from Switzerland – which meant he might recognise her. She paid him to hold up her guests with a gun. She poured water on the frayed lamp lead to blow the fuse, went out of the door, shot Rudi, cut herself with scissors and returned to the party.

Did you get it right?

5. One thing you may notice as you read more detective fiction: the murderer is often the person least likely to have committed the crime. Why do crime writers do this?

6 Openings

It doesn't matter how carefully and cleverly a writer plots their detective story if nobody reads it. The opening of a story is like a menu. When you read the text on the menu on the right, the writer is trying to make you order that dish. When a writer writes the opening to a story, they are trying to tempt you to read on, to grab your attention and hold it.

A succulent piece of steak, smothered in a delicious sauce, with crisp French fries and plump, pan-fried mushrooms

Activity 1

1   Read this opening from a short story by Margery Allingham called *Three Is a Lucky Number*.

At five o'clock on a September afternoon Ronald Frederick Torbay was making preparations for his third murder. He was being very wary, forcing himself to go slowly because he was perfectly sane and was well aware of the dangers of carelessness.

A career of homicide got more chancy as one went on. That piece of information had impressed him as being true as soon as he had read it in a magazine article way back before his first marriage. Also, he realised, success was liable to go to a man's head, so he kept a tight hold on himself. He was certain he was infinitely more clever than most human beings but he did not dwell on the fact and as soon as he felt the old thrill at the sense of his power welling up inside him, he quelled it firmly.

2   The writer tries to intrigue the reader in lots of ways. Here are some of them:

- We are told the specific time at which this takes place: 5p.m.
- We are given the character's full name, including his middle name
- We are told that he has committed two murders already, and he is about to commit a third
- We are told Torbay is perfectly sane.

a   Add to this list. Write down three other ways in which the writer tries to intrigue us.

b   Choose three points from your list and the list above. Write a sentence explaining **why** each of these might intrigue the reader.

3   Now that you have read the opening two paragraphs of this story, what do you hope the rest of the story will tell you?

Activity 2

Write the opening paragraph of a detective story. In your paragraph:

- introduce a character or situation which the reader wants to find out more about
- include details to intrigue the reader and make them want to find out what happens next.

Remember: the more questions you make your reader want to ask, the more you will intrigue them.

Sharpen your skills · Articles

Articles are small words that go in front of nouns.
The is the definite article. *A* and *an* are indefinite articles. For example:

He caught the criminal the next day.
He caught a criminal the next day.

The article tells us whether the writer means a specific (definite) criminal – or any (indefinite) criminal.

1 Copy out the sentences, inserting the appropriate article in the gaps.

2 Now write an ending to the story but leave out the articles. Ask a partner to fill the gaps.

Smith hated ___ man he worked for. He bought ___ bottle of poison and broke into his employer's office one night. He opened ___ window and climbed through. He found himself in ___ kitchen. He poisoned ___ water in ___ kettle. He poisoned ___ sugar bowl and ___ milk jug.

Assess your progress

1 Look at a partner's opening paragraph from Activity 2 while they look at your paragraph.
   a What questions does it make you ask about the character and the situation described? Write a list.
   b Which questions do you hope the rest of the story will answer?
   c Whose list has the most questions? Whose opening paragraph is the most intriguing?
   d Use this table to decide which level you and your partner are working at:

Level 4	Level 5	Level 6
I have given information about a character and a situation	Some information in my opening will make the reader ask questions	Almost all the information in my opening was selected to intrigue the reader

2 Look back to your work on the plot of Agatha Christie's *A Murder is Announced* on pages 68 and 69. Write a set of instructions for detective fiction writers. You could begin like this:

How To Plot A Murder Mystery
Phase one: the set-up
First, introduce your characters.
Then describe a murder.
Make sure that each of your characters has a motive for killing the victim!

Assessment task
Reading: Understanding the author's craft

Devices and Desires and *Fire Sale*

Your task
Read the opening from a detective novel called *Devices and Desires* by P.D. James and complete the activities that follow.

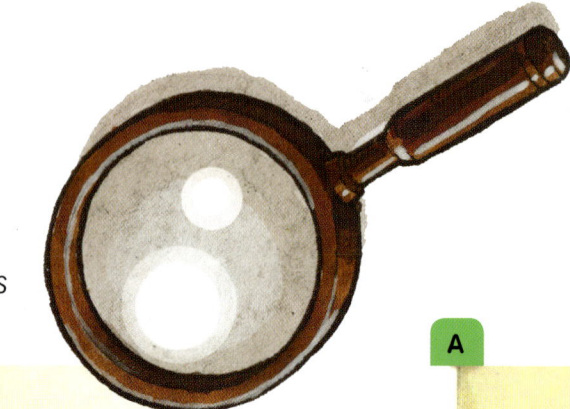

A

Devices and Desires

The Whistler's fourth victim was his youngest, Valerie Mitchell, aged fifteen years, eight months and four days, and she died because she missed the nine-forty bus from Easthaven to Cobb's Marsh. As always she had left it until the last minute to leave the disco and the floor was still a packed, gyrating mass of bodies under the makeshift strobe lights when she broke free of Wayne's clutching hands, shouted instructions to Shirl about their plans for next week above the raucous beat of the music and left the dance floor. Her last glimpse of Wayne was of his serious, bobbing face bizarrely striped with red, yellow and blue under the turning lights. Without waiting to change her shoes, she snatched up her jacket from the cloakroom peg and raced up the road past the darkened shops towards the bus station, her cumbersome shoulder bag flapping against her ribs. But when she turned the corner into the station she saw with horror that the lights on their high poles shone down on a bleached and silent emptiness and dashing to the corner was in time to see the bus already half-way up the hill. There was still a chance if the lights were against it and she began desperately chasing after it, hampered by her fragile, high-heeled shoes. But the lights were green and she watched helplessly, gasping and bent double with a sudden cramp, as it lumbered over the brow of a hill and like a brightly lit ship sank out of sight. 'Oh no!' she screamed after it, 'Oh God! Oh no!' and felt the tears of anger and dismay smarting her eyes.

This was the end. It was her father who laid down the rules in her family and there was never any appeal, any second chance. After protracted discussion and her repeated pleas she had been allowed this weekly visit on Friday evenings to the disco run by the church youth club, provided she caught the nine-forty bus without fail. It put her down at the Crown and Anchor at Cobb's Marsh, only fifty yards from her cottage. From ten fifteen her father would begin watching for the bus to pass the front room where he and her mother would sit half watching the television, the curtains drawn back. Whatever the programme or weather, he would then put on his coat and come out to walk the fifty yards to meet her, keeping her always in sight. Since the Norfolk Whistler had begun his killings her father had had an added justification for the mild domestic tyranny which, she half realised, he both thought right in dealing with his only child and rather enjoyed. The concordat had been early established: 'You do right by me, my girl, and I'll do right by you.' She both loved him and slightly feared him and she dreaded his anger. Now there would be one of those awful rows in which she knew she couldn't hope to look to her mother for support. It would be the end of her Friday evenings with Wayne and Shirl and the gang. Already they teased and pitied her because she was treated as a child. Now it would be total humiliation.

Explanation

concordat pact or agreement

1 How does the writer try to engage the reader's interest in the very first sentence of the book?

2 What does the writer's choice of language suggest the disco was like?

Refer to specific words and phrases used to describe the disco and comment on them.

…the floor was still a packed, gyrating mass of bodies under the makeshift strobe lights when she broke free of Wayne's clutching hands, shouted instructions to Shirl about their plans for next week above the raucous beat of the music and left the dance floor. Her last glimpse of Wayne was of his serious, bobbing face bizarrely striped with red, yellow and blue under the turning lights.

3 How does the section from 'As always…' to '…smarting her eyes.' build up a sense of Valerie's increasing anxiety about being late home?

Support your ideas by referring to this section.

4 What impression do you get of Valerie's father from this extract?

Complete the table below, identifying relevant quotations and commenting on what they suggest about Valerie's father.

Quotation from the extract	What this quotation suggests about Valerie's father

5 What do you think is going to happen next in the novel? Give reasons for your answer.

6 This extract ends with the line 'Now it would be total humiliation.' What effect might this sentence have on the reader's view of Valerie?

Now read the opening from a detective novel called *Fire Sale* by Sara Paretsky, which follows a private investigator making enquiries, and complete the activities that follow.

Fire Sale

I was halfway down the embankment when I saw the red-orange flash. I dropped to the ground and covered my head with my arms. And felt a pain in my shoulder so intense I couldn't even cry out.

Lying facedown in bracken and trash, I breathed in shallow panting breaths, a dog, eyes glazed, until the pain receded enough that I could move. I edged away from the flames on my hands and knees, then drew myself up on my knees and sat very still. I willed my breaths to come slow and deep, pushing the pain far enough away to manage it. Finally, I gingerly put a hand to my left shoulder. A stick. Metal or glass, some piece of the window that had shot out like an arrow from a crossbow. I tugged on the stick, but that sent such a river of agony flowing through me that I started to black out. I curled over, cradling my head on my knees.

When the wave subsided, I looked across at the factory. The back window that had blown apart was awash with fire, blue-red now, a mass so thick I couldn't make out flames, just a blur of hot colour. Bolts of fabric were stored there, fuelling the blaze.

And Frank Zamar. I remembered him with a sudden appalled jolt. Where had he been when that fireball blew up? I pushed myself to my feet as best I could and stumbled forward.

Weeping with pain, I pulled out my picklocks and tried to scrabble my way into the lock. It wasn't until my third futile attempt that I remembered my cell phone. I fumbled it out of my pocket and called 911.

While I waited on the fire trucks, I kept trying the lock. The stabbing in my left shoulder made it hard for me to manoeuvre the thin wards. I tried to brace them with my left hand, but my whole left side was shaking; I couldn't hold the picklocks steady.

I hadn't expected the fire – I hadn't expected anything when I came here. It was only some pricking of unease – dis-ease – that sent me back to Fly the Flag on my way home. I'd actually made the turn onto Route 41 when I decided to check on the factory. I'd made a U-turn onto Escanaba and zigzagged across the broken streets to South Chicago Avenue. It was six o'clock then, already dark, but I could see a handful of cars in Fly the Flag's yard when I drove by. There weren't any pedestrians out, not that there are ever many down here; only a few cars straggled past, beaters, people leaving the few standing factories to head for bars or even home.

I left my Mustang on one of the side streets, hoping it wouldn't attract any roving punk's attention. I tucked my cell phone and wallet into my coat pockets, took my picklocks from the glove compartment, and locked my bag in the trunk.

Explanation

ward part of a lock

Under cover of the cold November night, I scrambled up the embankment behind the plant, the steep hill that lifts the toll road over the top of the old neighbourhood. The roar of traffic on the Skyway above me blocked any sounds I made – including my own squawk when I caught my foot in a discarded tyre and tumbled hard to the ground.

From my perch under the expressway I could see the back entrance and the side yard, but not the front of the plant. When the shift ended at seven, I could just make out the shapes of people plodding to the bus stop. A few cars bumped behind them down the potholed drive to the road.

Lights were still on at the north end of the plant. One of the basement windows facing me also showed a pale fluorescent glow. If Frank Zamar were still on the premises, he could be doing something – anything – from checking inventory to planting dead rats in the vents. I wondered if I could find a crate in the rubble that would get me high enough to see into the back. I was halfway down the hillside, searching through the debris, when the window went briefly dark, then burst into fiery life.

1 How does the writer try to interest the reader in the story in the first paragraph?

2 Explain how the writer's choice of language helps to convey a sense of the pain she is in. Refer to specific words and phrases from paragraphs 1–6 and comment on them.

3 This novel is set in America. Complete the table below, identifying some features which suggest that the novel is set in America. Explain why each point suggests this.

Features which suggest that this novel is set in America	Why these features suggest this

4 What impression do you get of the narrator (the person telling the story) in this extract? Support your ideas by referring to the text.

5 What do you notice about the order in which the writer tells us about the story's events?

6 What do you think is going to happen next in the novel? Give reasons for your answer.

7 Now look again at **both** extracts. They are both from detective novels.

Compare the ways these two extracts try to provide a dramatic and exciting opening for the reader. You should comment on:
- who is telling the story and the effect this has on the reader
- where the story starts
- similarities and differences between the ways these two extracts are written
- which novel you would be more interested in reading and why.

7 Building description

You are learning:
● to develop your description when writing a detective story.

According to Van Dine's rules, detective fiction 'should contain no long descriptive passages'. Although description is not as important as plot in this genre, it is still needed to build a picture, to build tension and to engage the reader in the story.

Activity 1

1   Read this extract from *A Murder Is Announced*. The residents of Little Paddocks and the villagers of Chipping Cleghorn have gathered in Letitia Blacklock's drawing room to witness a murder which, according to a newspaper advert, is due to take place at 6.30p.m. Suddenly the lights go out.

> 'It's beginning,' cried Mrs Hamon in an ecstasy. Dora Bunner's voice cried out plaintively, 'Oh, I don't like it!' Other voices said, 'How terribly, terribly frightening!' 'It gives me the creeps.' 'Archie, where are you?' 'What do I have to *do*?' 'Oh dear – did I step on your foot? I'm sorry.'
>
> Then there was a crash, the door swung open. A powerful flashlight played rapidly round the room. A man's hoarse nasal voice, reminiscent to all of pleasant afternoons at the cinema, directed the company crisply to:
>
> 'Stick 'em up!'
>
> 'Stick 'em up, I tell you!' the voice barked.
>
> Delightedly, hands were raised willingly above heads.
>
> 'Isn't it wonderful?' breathed a female voice. 'I'm *so* thrilled.'
>
> And then, unexpectedly, a revolver spoke. It spoke twice. The ping of two bullets shattered the complacency of the room. Suddenly the game was no longer a game.
>
> Someone screamed…
>
> The figure in the doorway whirled suddenly round, it seemed to hesitate, a third shot rang out, it crumpled and then it crashed to the ground. The flashlight dropped and went out.
>
> There was darkness once again. And gently, with a little Victorian protesting moan, the drawing-room door, as was its habit when not properly open, swung gently to and latched with a click.

2   Compare the language at the start of the extract with that at the end of the extract:

ecstasy   delighted   wonderful   shattered   crumpled   crashed

a   Why do you think the author, Agatha Christie, has used this contrast?

b A lot of characters speak in the first paragraph but only two are named – most of the dialogue is not attributed to a character. What effect is Christie trying to create here?

c The gunman's voice is described as being 'reminiscent to all of pleasant afternoons at the cinema'. What is Christie suggesting with this comparison?

3 Re-read these sentences from the extract:

> And then, unexpectedly, a revolver spoke. It spoke twice.

Christie has used personification and repetition to describe the gunshots. Why?

4 Re-read the final sentence of the extract.
a Thinking back to the plot summary on pages 68–69, why has Christie described the door closing?
b Why has Christie ended her description with this quiet, everyday occurrence?

Activity 2

1 Choose one of the following titles:

2 Write two paragraphs for your chosen title describing a murder. Try to use the same descriptive techniques as Agatha Christie. Tick them off as you plan and write.

Contrast ☐
Unattributed dialogue ☐
Comparison ☐
Personification ☐
Repetition ☐
A low-key ending ☐

Assess your progress

1 Swap your descriptive writing with a partner. Can you identify where they have used the different techniques listed in Activity 2? Label their writing.

2 Now use this table to see which level you are working at in Reading and Writing.

	Level 4	Level 5	Level 6
Reading	I can identify most of the techniques	I can comment on most of the techniques	I can comment on all of the techniques and their effect
Writing	I can use one of these techniques	I can use some of these techniques	I can use most of these techniques

Sharpen your skills — Question marks

Read these sentences:

I am the greatest detective ever.
Am I the greatest detective ever?

The first is a statement; the second is a question. Turn the following statements into questions:

1 There are many clues to the murderer's identity.

2 He was very cleverly disguised.

3 We can catch him before he escapes.

8 Providing the clues

You are learning:
- to give clues in a detective story to engage the reader.

One of Van Dine's rules for a successful detective story is that 'the reader must have equal opportunity with the detective for solving the mystery'. To let the reader join in with the detective work, the writer must give the reader all the clues they need.

Activity 1

1 Read this extract from *A Case of Identity* by Arthur Conan Doyle. Mary Sutherland has come to Sherlock Holmes to find a missing person. She begins by describing her stepfather, Mr Windibank:

'I call him father, though it sounds funny, too, for he is only five years and two months older than myself.'

'And your mother is alive?'

'Oh, yes, mother is alive and well. I wasn't best pleased, Mr Holmes, when she married again so soon after father's death, and a man who was nearly fifteen years younger than herself. Father was a plumber, and he left a tidy business behind him, which mother carried on with Mr Hardy, the foreman; but when Mr Windibank came he made her sell the business. They got 4700 pounds for the goodwill and interest, which wasn't near as much as father could have got if he had been alive.'

I had expected to see Sherlock Holmes impatient under this rambling and inconsequential narrative, but, on the contrary he had listened with the greatest concentration of attention.

'Your own little income,' he asked, 'does it come out of the business?'

'Oh, no, sir. It is quite separate and was left me by my uncle Ned in Auckland. It is in New Zealand stock, paying 4½ per cent. Two thousand five hundred pounds was the amount, but I can only touch the interest. As I live at home I don't wish to be a burden to them, and so they have the use of the money just while I am staying with them. Mr Windibank draws my interest every quarter and pays it over to mother, and I find that I can do pretty well with what I earn at typewriting.'

'You have made your position very clear to me,' said Holmes. 'Kindly tell us now all about your connection with Mr Hosmer Angel.'

'I met him first at the gasfitters' ball,' she said. 'They used to send father tickets when he was alive, and then afterwards they remembered us, and sent them to mother. Mr Windibank did not wish us to go. At last, he went off to France upon the business of the firm, but we went, mother and I, with Mr Hardy, who used to be our foreman.'

'I suppose,' said Holmes, 'that when Mr Windibank came back from France he was very annoyed at your having gone to the ball.'

'Oh, well, he was very good about it. He laughed,

I remember, and shrugged his shoulders, and said there was no use denying anything to a woman.'

'I see. Then at the gasfitters' ball you met, as I understand, Mr Hosmer Angel.'

'Yes, sir. I met him that night, and he called next day to ask if we had got home all safe, and after that we met him – that is to say, Mr Holmes, I met him twice for walks, but after that father came back again, and Mr Hosmer Angel could not come to the house any more.'

'No?'

'Well, father was going off to France again in a week, and Hosmer wrote and said that it would be safer and better not to see each other until he had gone. We could write in the meantime, and he used to write every day. I took the letters in in the morning, so there was no need for father to know.'

'Can you remember any other little things about Mr Hosmer Angel?'

'He was a very shy man, Mr Holmes. He would rather walk with me in the evening than in the daylight, for he said that he hated to be conspicuous. Very retiring and gentlemanly he was. Even his voice was gentle. He'd had the quinsy and swollen glands when he was young, he told me, and it had left him with a weak throat, and a hesitating, whispering fashion of speech. He was always well dressed, very neat and plain, but his eyes were weak, just as mine are, and he wore tinted glasses against the glare.'

'What happened when Mr Windibank, your stepfather, returned to France?'

'Mr Hosmer Angel came to the house again and proposed that we should marry before father came back. He was in dreadful earnest and made me swear that whatever happened I would always be true to him. It was to be at St Saviour's, near King's Cross, and we were to have breakfast afterwards at the St Pancras Hotel. Hosmer came for us in a hansom, but as there were two of us he put us both into it and stepped himself into a four-wheeler, which happened to be the only other cab in the street. We got to the church first, and when the four-wheeler drove up we waited for him to step out, but he never did, and when the cabman got down from the box and looked there was no one there! That was last Friday, Mr Holmes, and I have never seen or heard anything since then to throw any light upon what became of him.'

Explanations

stock **money invested**
hansom/four-wheeler **horse and carriage**

a What do you think has happened to Hosmer Angel?

Here is the solution to the mystery:

> Hosmer Angel is in fact Mr Windibank in disguise. He has done this so that his stepdaughter will not marry anyone else – she will stay at home and Windibank will keep getting the money she gives him. Holmes explains:
>
> 'James Windibank wished Miss Sutherland to be so bound to Hosmer Angel that for ten years she would not listen to another man. As far as the church door he brought her, and then, as he could go no farther, he conveniently vanished away by the old trick of stepping in at one door of a four-wheeler and out at the other.'

b Now that you know the solution, re-read the extract. Identify as many clues as you can which might help the reader to solve the mystery.

c *Red herrings* are false clues put in by the writer to mislead the reader and keep the solution secret until the end of the story. Can you spot any in this story?

9 Planning a story

You are learning:

● to plan a detective story featuring all key elements of the genre.

Planning is the most important stage in any piece of writing. With planning, you will produce a text that will hold the reader's attention and interest. Without planning, you will produce a text that starts, goes on for a while and then stops.

Activity 1

Planning is probably more important in writing a successful piece of detective fiction than in any other text.

Below are the ingredients for the detective genre. Organise them in a flowchart or spidergram to show how they all fit together to create a murder mystery story.

Hint: You may find it helpful to refer back to the instructions you wrote in the Assess your progress section on page 71: How To Plot A Murder Mystery.

c **Some suspects**

a **A detective**

b **A victim**

d **Some witnesses**

e **A setting: time and place**

f **A murder**

g **Some clues**

EXHIBIT A

EXHIBIT B

h **Some red herrings**

i **A solution**

Activity 2

Use a table like the one below to plan your own detective story.

The victim is:	
The murderer is:	
The murderer killed the victim because:	
The murderer killed the victim by:	
The setting for the story is:	
The other suspects are:	They might have wanted to kill the victim too because:
	1
	2
	3
The detective is:	
The clues that give the murderer away are: ● ● ●	
The red herrings that will mislead the reader are: ● ●	
The final clue that leads the detective to the murderer is:	

Sharpen your skills Conditionals

Conditional verbs are modal verbs used when talking or writing about possibilities. Read these three examples:

● If the detective is quick, he will catch the killer.
● If the killer handled this gun, there would be fingerprints.
● If the gun had been fired, we would have heard the shots.

Match these halves together to make three sentences that use conditionals correctly:

1	If you lend me some money	A	I would do my homework.
2	If it didn't take so long	B	I will pay you back next week.
3	If I had some money	C	I would lend it to you.

Using these examples, try to work out the rules for using conditionals.

Assessment task
Writing: Composition and conventions

Are you the next Agatha Christie?

A big publisher is running a detective story writing competition.

This is the notice they send out:

> ### Calling all budding writers!
> **We are looking for exciting and dramatic openings of detective stories, which will really grab readers' attention and interest.**
>
> In particular, we are looking for –
> - a really dramatic first couple of paragraphs, which take the reader straight into the action
> - an explanation of what happened to lead up to that point in which the setting and the characters are introduced
> - a distinctive narrative voice or style.

Your task

Write your opening of a detective story for the competition.

Remember to:
- choose words and phrases deliberately to create particular effects
- use paragraphs of different lengths and link them in a variety of ways
- proof-read your writing to make sure it is clear and accurate.

4 Communication

Objectives

In this unit you will:

Reading
- Identify how different texts are organised and laid out, and what effect this creates
- consider how different audiences might respond to texts
- express preferences and opinions about texts.

Composition
- plan your writing so that you develop strong arguments
- use paragraphs correctly to sequence your ideas
- write a variety of arguments, both for and against an issue, and from a balanced point of view.

Conventions
- learn how and why writers use different degrees of formality and informality
- develop your knowledge of grammar, including how and when to use first and third person and active and passive voice.

Language
- read texts from a range of historical periods, showing how language has changed over time.

By the end of this unit you will:
- read and answer questions on a variety of articles about space exploration (Reading: Reading for meaning)
- write a review of a television programme you loathe (Writing: Composition and conventions).

Cross-curricular links
- **ICT**
  Communicating information; Impact of technology: Social, ethical and cultural implications
- **Citizenship**
  Critical thinking and enquiry: Issues and problems
- **History**
  Chance and continuity
- **Science**
  Applications and implications of science

1 Communication forms

You are learning:

● to recognise how different types of communication are organised and understand how ICT has influenced the style of language.

Many new forms of communication have become popular in the twenty-first century. ICT means that we can keep in touch with others more easily, for work and leisure.

We need to:

● be aware of the new language and vocabulary associated with these new forms
● understand how to communicate in these different media
● recognise both the advantages and risks of these new forms.

Activity 1

1 How many of the communication forms below are you familiar with?

2 Which of the communication forms below do you think are new and were not available to previous generations – for example your parents and grandparents – when they were teenagers?

● wiki
● instant messaging/SMS
● radio
● email
● blogs
● websites
● TV advertisements
● newspapers
● social networking sites
● mail
● phone

a Which communication form do you think is the slowest?
b Which communication form is the quickest?
c Identify any terms that you are not familiar with and find out what they mean. You could use the Internet or ask others.
d What advantages do you think these new forms of communication give your generation that were not available to your grandparents?

Activity 2

Social networking sites are a popular way of communicating and exchanging information. MySpace is an example of a social networking site, while Facebook defines itself as a social utility that connects users with the buld people around them. It has been said that these sites have been used to make famous people ordinary and ordinary people famous! The singer Lily Allen launched her career using MySpace.

1   Look at the text below from Facebook. Look carefully at the organisational features of this page – for example images, links, menus, colour, headings. Write a sentence for each one, explaining why you think it has been used and how effective you think it is.

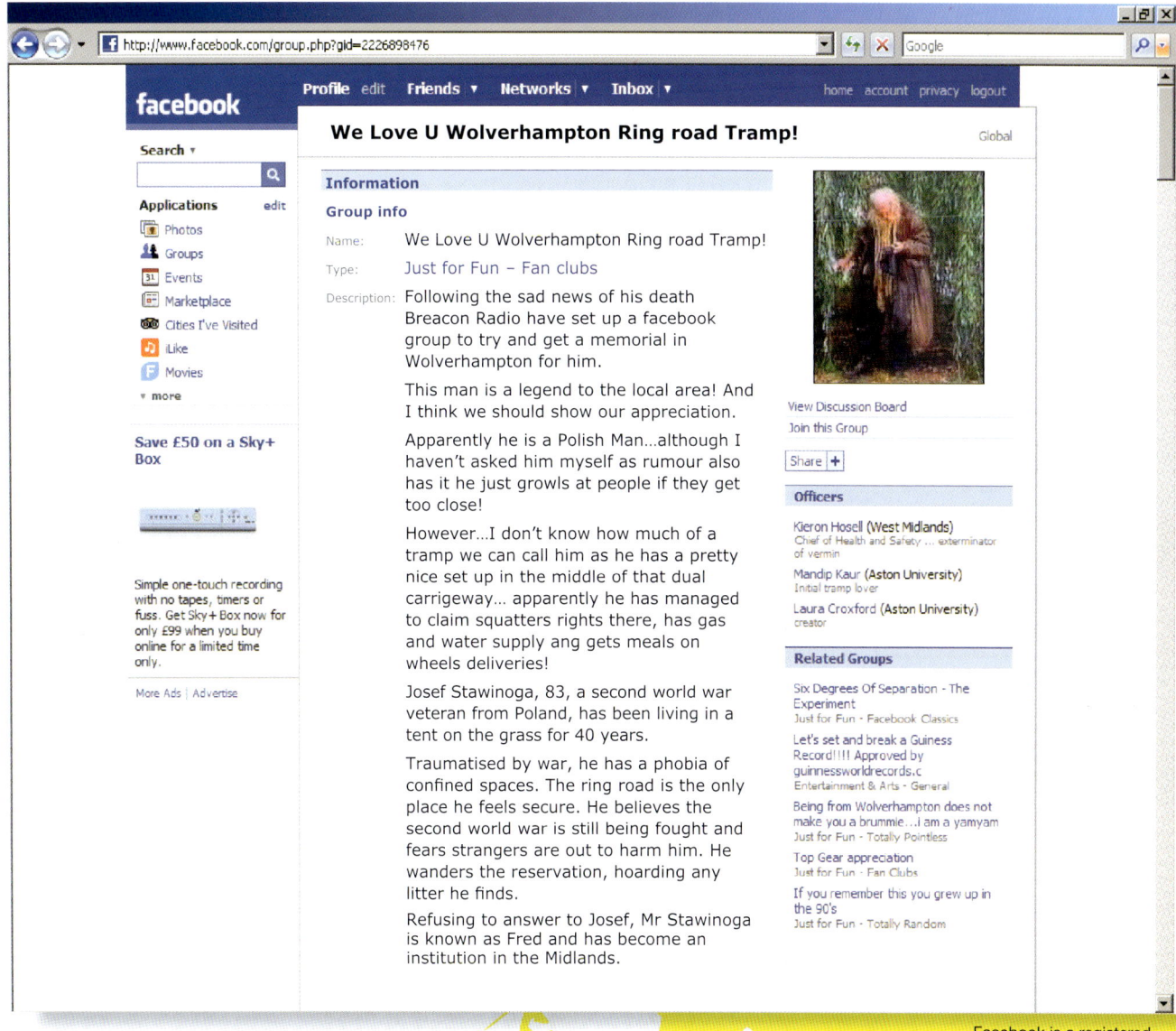

Josef Stawinoga – the Wolverhampton Ringroad Tramp

Facebook is a registered trademark of Facebook, Inc.

Assess your progress

You are learning to identify how texts such as social networking pages are organised. Decide which level you are working at and what your target for improvement is.

Level 4	Level 5	Level 6
I can identify and describe some organisational features of different texts	I can identify organisational features of different texts and explain why they have been used	I can identify organisational features of different texts and make comments about their effectiveness

85

2 Safety and communication

You are learning:
● to select key points from your reading.

As the Internet has allowed young people to widen their networks of communication, safety issues have become increasingly important.

Activity 1

1 Read the extract below from an article advising young people about Internet safety.

   a What is the difference between the black text and the red text in this article?

   b What is the purpose of paragraph 1 of this article?

   c What potential risks does this article highlight for young people who use the Internet? Summarise these in bullet points. For example, what does the article suggest you need to be aware of when using chatrooms?

Directgov
www.direct.gov.uk
Public services all in one place

Cymraeg | Accessibility | Help | Site index

Search the site   Go ➡

Home | Directories | Guide to Govt | Do it online | Newsroom

Browse by subject
▸ Crime, justice and the law
▸ Education and learning
▸ Employment
▸ Environment and greener living
▸ Health and well-being
▸ Home and community
▸ Money, tax and benefits
▸ Motoring
▸ Rights and responsibilites
▸ Travel and transport

Browse by people
▸ Young people
▾ Crime and justice
  ▾ Keeping safe
▸ Britons living abroad
▸ Caring for someone
▸ Disabled people
▸ Over 50s

Young people

Staying safe online

It's important that if you're using the internet, you know how to stay safe. You should never give out any personal information when you're online, no matter who you think you're talking to.

Using the internet

There are loads of sites around that allow you to talk to other people on the web. Chat rooms give you the chance to have a conversation with other people and get instant replies, while online message boards let you post up questions or comments and ask other users to give their opinion in their own time.

It can be a great way to chat to other people who share your interests, but you should always be careful not to pass on any of your personal details. You should always keep in mind that internet users can pretend to be anyone they like. They can lie about their age, their interests and whether they're male or female. No matter how long you've been chatting, remember that they're still strangers; you don't really know them at all.

Find out more about cyberbullying (opens new window)

Social networking sites

Some of you may have your own web page set up that lets you chat with friends or communicate with other users who share your interests. These 'social networks' also let you create your own blog, upload photos and videos for others to see, and add people to an online friends list.

Social networks are a great way of keeping in touch but you should think carefully before adding someone to your list of online friends or posting a blog entry that could get you into trouble at school, college or work. Remember that:

● your page is still a public place, so putting anything on your page that you wouldn't want your parents, teacher or boss to see is not a good idea
● you can never be sure that other users are being truthful about their online identities, so be careful about what information you give out
● think about whether you know someone well enough before accepting them into your group of linked friends

● make sure you know who to contact to report abuse or bullying on your page and how your complaint will be dealt with
● If you are looking for more information about staying in control of your page and how to get the most out of social networking sites, ThinkUKnow has all the advice you need.

Advice on social networks, blogs and file sharing from ThinkUKnow (opens new window)

Chat room safety

To stay safe, make sure that when you're using a chat room or posting on a message board, you never give out any personal information like your address or your phone number. You should always use a nickname, so no-one can look you up in a telephone directory and get your home phone number.

It's usually not a good idea to arrange to meet up with someone that you've been chatting to online. Remember that you can never be sure that they're telling the truth about their age or their interests and you could be putting yourself in danger.

Read about the dangers of online chatrooms (opens new window)
Top tips on staying safe online (opens new window)

Personal details

Some websites will ask you to fill out a registration form before you can use them. While this is normal practice, it's a good idea to find out what the website will do with your personal details. All companies that collect information have to tell their customers how personal information will be used. Make sure you check the website's terms and conditions if you want to know.

Activity 2

Comment on the writer's language choices and their effect in the quotations below.

a 'No matter how long you've been chatting, remember that they're still strangers; you don't really know them at all.'
Comment on the purpose of the semi-colon in this sentence.

b Comment on why the writer uses imperative verbs in the phrases below.
'be careful about what information you give out'
'think about whether you know someone well enough'

c 'It's usually not a good idea to arrange to meet up with someone you've been chatting to online.'
Why do you think the writer has used the word 'usually'? How would the writer's advice be changed without this word?

Activity 3

Copy the table below and complete it using relevant information from the article.

Key advice when providing personal details on the Internet	Key advice when using social networking sites	Key advice when using chatrooms
Find out how the information will be used	Be careful about what personal information you share	Avoid arranging face-to-face meetings

Activity 4

1 Using the advice in the table above, write a paragraph for your school newsletter, giving three key pieces of advice about home Internet use.

2 Of these three pieces of advice, which do you think is the most important for your age group?

Sharpen your skills First and third person

The first person is used to refer to yourself, for example, 'I am a student'. The third person is used to refer to someone or something else, for example, 'He is in Year 11'.

1 Why has the social networking page on page 85 been written in the third person?

2 Rewrite the last three paragraphs of the 'description section' of the Facebook extract so they are in the first person.

3 Privacy and communication

You are learning:
- to recognise how writers organise features of a text.

In some new areas of communication, such as text-messaging and social networking, teenagers have been one of the fastest-growing user groups. Teenagers have been active in creating their own cultures and languages as part of this use.

Read the newspaper extract below that reviews a variety of parents' opinions about this.

How far would you go?

She's 14, looks 18, and is full of attitude. You want to find out what's going on in her world... Sophie Radice talks to parents who snoop on their teens' cyber secrets

The Guardian, Saturday October 20, 2007

Victoria, 50, from Hampshire, has four daughters aged between nine and 18

'You're not a good parent if you don't know what your kids are doing. In what other part of their life do you just sign off responsibility and leave them to cope on their own? In a casual way, I check their Bebo sites, their mobiles and look in their address books in their mobiles to make sure that everything is OK and that things are not getting out of hand. I am pretty good at teen speak now and I can tell any parent who wants to know.

'My kids are aware that I do a bit of light monitoring and seem pretty used to it by now. I can reassure parents who wouldn't dream of prying that most of what goes on is pretty dull. At first I was really shocked by the photos they put up and then I realised that, particularly on MSN and MySpace, they create wilder, more interesting personas that often bear little relation to who they are and what they are really doing. It's often quite funny and creative and they really listen to each other's music and poetry.'

Jane, 39, from south-east London, has two sons aged six and 15

'I wouldn't have even thought of going through my son's things, until he started staying out without telling me where he was. I had quite a few nights last summer when I rang around hospitals, police stations, and all his friends trying to find him. When he came home he didn't seem to care how scared I was. He still won't tell me where he is and just turns off his phone.

'I'm a single mum and I feel that I have to find new ways to find out what is going on, and so if I can go through his phone when he has put it down or have a look at what he is writing on his MSN then I will. That way I find out where he has been, what he is planning and who he is seeing.'

Richard, 57, from Exeter, has three daughters aged 25, 23 and 19

'My youngest daughter was on my laptop and left her email on the screen, which I happened to see was from my middle daughter, who is at university. She talked a lot about how much she is drinking and about not doing any work and also said something slightly derogatory about my wife, which was a bit unkind, although not serious. I didn't think much of it so said casually to my youngest daughter that I had seen it and that she was lucky to have heard from her. Well, it completely blew up in my face because my youngest daughter said that we had always taught them to respect other people's property and there I was just looking at private stuff and who did I think I was? Some patriarch who thought he had the right to snoop?

'I had my wife and all my daughters completely livid with me. I did try to say that it was just left up there for me to see and that I would have to have had no interest in my daughters whatsoever not to read something that was right in front of me.'

Activity 1

1   This article is taken from the 'Family' section of the *Guardian* weekend newspaper. Who is the intended reader for this text?

2   List the different opinions that are offered by parents about checking on their teenagers and decide where each parent's name should go on the chart below:

Parents should
not check

Parents should
definitely check

3   **a**   Write a sentence summing up each parent's attitude to checking on their teenagers.
    b   What do you think about the opinions of the parents in the article?
    c   Select one quotation from each parent that you either agree with or disagree with. Write a comment next to each quotation expressing your point of view.
    d   How do you think different audiences might respond to this text? For example, adults who have children, adults who don't, teenagers and so on.

Activity 2

Writers make choices about presentational features in order to engage their readers. Look at the presentational features of the newspaper article on page 88 (the image, text formatting and colour) and answer the questions below.

1   How might the image catch the interest of the intended reader?

2   How is text formatting such as emboldening and different font sizes used to structure the article and interest the reader in the examples that follow?

Victoria, 50, from Hampshire, has four daughters aged between nine and 18

She's 14, looks 18, and is full of attitude.

How far would you go?

Activity 3

Look at the quotations below and comment on how language is used to interest the reader.

'You want to find out what's going on in her world'

'How far would you go?'

'parents who snoop on their teens' cyber secrets'

Activity 4

Both the articles on pages 86 and 88 highlight some of the dangers of modern communications for young people.

1   Consider the differences between the style and content of the two articles, by copying out the table below and inserting the correct terms from the word bank. An example has been filled in for you.

Feature	'Staying safe online'	*Guardian* 'Family' article
Intended audience		
Purpose	writing to advise	
Language style		
Presentational features	• • •	• • •

formal	images	different font sizes
less formal	emboldened text	coloured text
parents	headings	writing to advise
young people	headlines	writing to entertain

2   Now choose two features from the four listed above and write a paragraph to contrast the two texts, using examples to support your points. Remember to comment on how the features you have chosen contribute to the texts' meaning and purpose.

Sharpen your skills Active and passive voice

Most of the time, we use the active voice when we write and speak. It tells us who (or what) did what to who (or what). So this sentence, which is in the active voice…

'You impressed me.' …tells us what you did to me.

The passive voice does not always tell us who did the action – it focuses on the person who was affected by it. So in this sentence, which is in the passive voice, we are only told about what happened – not who did it.

I was impressed.

1   Identify which of the three sentences below use the passive voice and which use the active voice.
   a   You should never give out any personal information.
   b   My kids are aware that I do a bit of light monitoring.
   c   At first I was really shocked by the photos they put up.

2   Choose a sentence from question 1 which is written in the active voice, and rewrite it using the passive voice.

Assess your progress

Look at your responses to Activity 4 on page 90. How confident did you feel comparing the two texts? Use the table below to identify the level of your reading skills.

Level 4	Level 5	Level 6
• I can identify the audience and purpose of a text • I can make some comments on the presentational and language features in a text	• I can explain how the presentational and language features of a text have been chosen to suit the audience and purpose	• I can comment on how the presentational and language features of a text have been chosen to suit the audience and purpose, and the effect the writer is trying to create

4 Formal and informal communication

You are learning:

● to identify the features of formal and informal texts.

Another popular modern form of communication is the blog. Many social networking pages or personal webpages contain links to blogs. A blog (web log) is a website where entries are written in chronological order. Many provide commentary or news on a particular subject; others function as more personal online diaries. A typical blog combines text, images, and links to other blogs, webpages, and other media related to its topic.

Activity 1

Read the three diary entries below and opposite, then link each one to its correct author and decide whether it is a blog or a handwritten diary. Give reasons for your choices.

Explanation

chronological order **time order: the order in which things happen**

(a) Moby (born Richard Melville Hall, 11 September 1965) is an American songwriter, musician and singer, well known for his political and environmental beliefs.

(b) Samuel Pepys (23 February 1633 – 26 May 1703) was an English naval administrator and Member of Parliament. He is now most famous for his diary, which describes historical events such as the Great Plague and the Great Fire of London.

(c) Steve Alton is a children's novelist and illustrator, author of fantasy fiction including *The Malifex, Finlay and the Bogeyman* and *The Firehills*.

Text 1

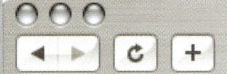
saturday

on saturday i'm going upstate to an animal sanctuary where, in theory, i'll be able to play with pigs and cows that have been rescued from those happy places where they torture and kill pigs and cows. have i mentioned that i'm a vegan...? here's my simple request...
in a perfect world animals would not suffer for human purposes. but we don't live in a perfect world. in a perfect world we'd all be vegans. again, we don't live in a perfect world. i'm not going to be presumptuous and tell you that you should be a vegan or a vegetarian. what i will ask is that you ask yourself the question:
'could i look into an animal's eyes and say: my hunger is more important than your suffering?' let your conscience be your guide. if you do choose to eat meat and/or dairy products could you at least consider eating compassionately farmed meat and/or dairy? ...thanks for listening,

Text 2

File   Edit   View   Favorites   Tools   Help

Address   Go   Links »

FRIDAY, OCTOBER 19, 2007

Hot cakes

Well, The Gooey, Chewy, Rumble, Plop Book seems to be selling very well – apparently it has sold out its first print run in the UK and is likely to do the same in several other countries.

So get a copy quickly, while you still can!

Work is progressing well on the sequel, which I think is going to be just as good...

POSTED AT 10:48 AM 0 COMMENTS

WEDNESDAY, AUGUST 02, 2006

Job's a good 'un!

Well, I've finished the first draft text of volume 1 in the 'Gorgeously Gross Guides' series, and it has passed the first editing hurdle with flying colours. We're now choosing microscope photos of various unpleasant bits of the human body for a 'guess the close-up' feature on each page.

I'm quietly confident that it's going to be a blinder when it's finished!

[feeling: smug]

POSTED AT 4.02 PM 0 COMMENTS

Text 3

January 28, 1661
To the Theatre, where I saw again
'The Lost Lady,' which do now please
me better than before; and here I sitting
in a dark place, a lady spit backward
upon me by a mistake, not seeing me; but
after seeing her to be a very pretty lady,
I was not troubled at it at all.

Activity 2

Blogs are generally characterised by informal language and informal style.

1   How many different examples of this can you find in Text 1?
    Complete the list below:

- no capital letters at the beginning of sentences
- contractions such as *I'm, don't.*

2   Pick two informal sentences from this blog and rewrite them
    in a very formal style.

Activity 3

Like a personal diary, a blog is a place where a person can reveal
much about their character, thoughts and lifestyle. What do you
learn about the character, thoughts and lifestyle of the writer from
Text 1? Use examples and quotations to support your points.
You might use the sentence starters below to help you.

What we learn	quotations
We learn about Moby's lifestyle through his comments about food...	have i mentioned that i'm a vegan...?
We learn that Moby is not shy about speaking about his political views...	
We learn that Moby is a sociable musician who is using his blog to talk to his fans...	

 **Sharpen your skills** **Exclamations**

Exclamation marks can be used when someone cries out, gives an order,
shouts, or says something forcefully or humorously.

Look at this modernised
version of Pepys' diary
entry on page 93.

> I went to the theatre where I saw 'The Lost Lady' again. I enjoyed
> it more this time than last time. I was sitting in a dark place
> and a lady, not seeing me, spat backwards onto me by mistake.
> I was not troubled by it at all once I realised she was very pretty.

Choose the two best places where you could replace a full stop with an
exclamation mark. Then compare your results with a partner's and discuss
the reasons for your answers. How would putting the exclamation marks in a
different place change the meaning of those sentences?

Assessment task

Reading: Reading for meaning

Holidays in space – a good idea or not?

Read texts A–D on pages 95–7.

Text A

Logotron :: Article – Holidays in Space

http://www.logo.com/newsletter/11/holidays.htm

Logotron
educational software

Partners with the teaching profession - Pioneers in Learning

home / about / products / support / my cart / search

Holidays in space

On May 25, 1961, President Kennedy first voiced a goal, 'before this decade is out, of landing a man on the moon and returning him safely to the earth'. It captured the public imagination. It was like Columbus all over again and you felt you were riding on the crest of a wave of human achievement.

National pride had its part to play, of course. The Space Race was essentially between the two great superpowers, America and Russia, and everyone supported one side or the other as if it were a global football competition.

The culmination, as everybody knows, was Neil Armstrong, who on 21st July 1969 set foot on the moon for the first time ever and uttered those immortal words, 'That's one small step for man but one giant leap for mankind.'

Everybody thought that by the end of the century we'd be taking holidays on the moon – or at the very least on a space station – but somehow this has never happened. After that first momentous landing, enthusiasm for space exploration seemed to slowly fizzle out. True, a few more astronauts walked on the moon, and there is a space shuttle which flies up and down regularly; there's even a half-built space station, but it's nothing like we imagined.

So what changed? Did we become bored with space? Did the shuttle disasters shake our faith in the value-versus-cost of space travel? Or did problems on earth get worse and make us try to sort out hunger and poverty before embarking on such a costly exercise as space exploration?

The answer is actually far more mundane than that and like many things, it all comes down to money.

Space exploration seems to be extortionately expensive. We see it as something quite different from anything that has happened before. The Wright brothers' first flight, for example, seems quite straightforward and inexpensive when compared to colonising the moon. Space travel, by contrast, can only happen if literally billions of dollars are poured into it – and that's something only the taxes of the very richest nations could ever finance.

Or so we think.

In fact, human flight was exactly the same as space flight in that it is a challenge which takes place at the very cutting edge of technology. There is no difference. The Wright brothers didn't need to be funded by a national programme paid by taxes and nor should space. If they had, we might still be waiting for the first package holiday to Spain instead of waiting for the first package holiday to the moon.

The Wright brothers used their own money to fund their experiments and eventually, as we all know, they succeeded at Kittyhawk in 1903. What we don't know is that their modern counterparts are doing exactly the same thing all over the world right now. Inventive and creative people are experimenting with the technology of space flight day in and day out and what's more, they're funding their work through raffles and barbeques!

Occasionally we see one of them in that last amusing sport on the news. They are usually shown as harmless eccentrics and we have a quiet chuckle before the next programme starts. But in reality, they are getting far closer than we think to solving some of the problems of space flight.

One thing that is driving their enthusiasm is the 'X Prize'. You may not have heard of it because it's not widely publicised. The X Prize is 'a $10,000,000 prize to jumpstart the space tourism industry through competition between the most talented entrepreneurs and rocket experts in the world.'

Text B

NASA – NASA's Newest Concept Vehicles Take Off-Roading Out of This World

http://www.nasa.gov/mission_pages/constellation/main/lunar_truck.html

| HOME | NEWS | MISSIONS | MULTIMEDIA | ABOUT NASA | › Help and Preferences |

Username   › Log In › Sign Up   Search

NASA Home | Missions | Constellation Program | Constellation Main   › Send   › Bookmark   › Print

Missions

Missions Highlights

▼ **Current Missions**
Current Missions
  Constellation Program
    Orion Crew Vehicle
    Ares Launch Vehicles
    Altair Lunar Lander
    Multimedia
    News & Media Resources
    Exploration Vision

Past Missions

Future Missions

Launch Schedule

Mission Calendar

Constellation
NASA's New Spacecraft: Ares and Orion

Feature

NASA's Newest Concept Vehicles Take Off-Roading Out of This World

In a car commercial, it would sound odd: active suspension, six-wheel drive with independent steering for each wheel, no doors, no windows, no seats and the only colour it comes in is gold.

But NASA's latest concept vehicle is meant to go way, way off-road – as in 240,000 miles from the nearest pavement, driving on the moon. NASA is working to send astronauts to the moon by 2020 to set up a lunar outpost, where they will do scientific research and prepare for journeys to destinations like Mars.

NASA is testing many technologies needed for research on the moon. Two examples are a lunar truck for astronauts and a rover equipped with a drill designed to dig into the moon's soil.

The concept for a future lunar truck was built at NASA's Johnson Space Center, Houston. The vehicle provides an idea of what the transportation possibilities may be when astronauts start exploring the moon. Other than a few basic requirements, the primary instruction given to the designers was to throw away assumptions made on NASA's previous rovers and come up with new ideas.

Text C

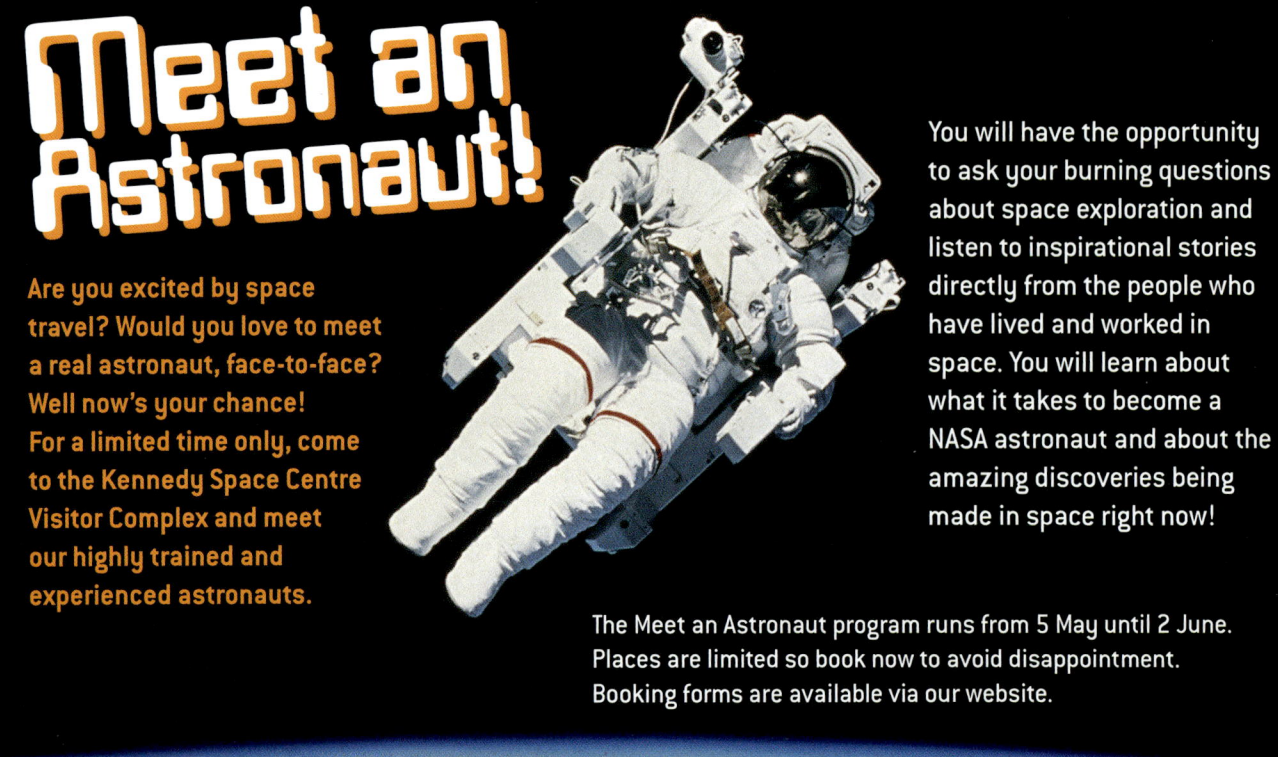

Meet an Astronaut!

**Are you excited by space travel? Would you love to meet a real astronaut, face-to-face? Well now's your chance!
For a limited time only, come to the Kennedy Space Centre Visitor Complex and meet our highly trained and experienced astronauts.**

You will have the opportunity to ask your burning questions about space exploration and listen to inspirational stories directly from the people who have lived and worked in space. You will learn about what it takes to become a NASA astronaut and about the amazing discoveries being made in space right now!

The Meet an Astronaut program runs from 5 May until 2 June. Places are limited so book now to avoid disappointment. Booking forms are available via our website.

Text D

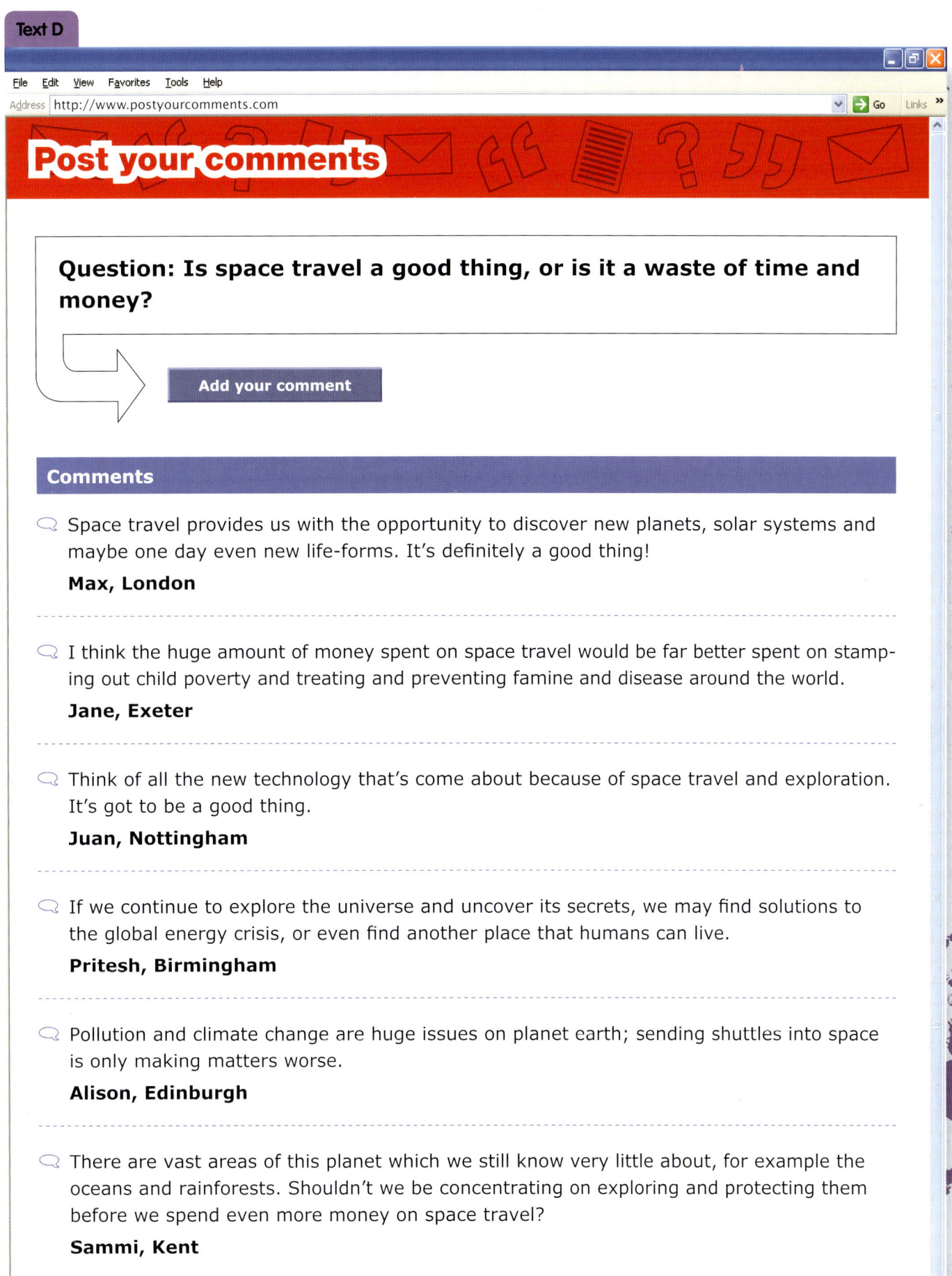

File   Edit   View   Favorites   Tools   Help

Address http://www.postyourcomments.com   Go   Links »

Post your comments

Question: Is space travel a good thing, or is it a waste of time and money?

Add your comment

Comments

Space travel provides us with the opportunity to discover new planets, solar systems and maybe one day even new life-forms. It's definitely a good thing!

Max, London

I think the huge amount of money spent on space travel would be far better spent on stamping out child poverty and treating and preventing famine and disease around the world.

Jane, Exeter

Think of all the new technology that's come about because of space travel and exploration. It's got to be a good thing.

Juan, Nottingham

If we continue to explore the universe and uncover its secrets, we may find solutions to the global energy crisis, or even find another place that humans can live.

Pritesh, Birmingham

Pollution and climate change are huge issues on planet earth; sending shuttles into space is only making matters worse.

Alison, Edinburgh

There are vast areas of this planet which we still know very little about, for example the oceans and rainforests. Shouldn't we be concentrating on exploring and protecting them before we spend even more money on space travel?

Sammi, Kent

Your task

1 Pick out the key events given in Text A and list them in chronological order.

2 The writer makes comparisons between events in the past and events related to space travel.

   a Complete the table below, identifying two pairs of events that are linked. One has been done for you:

Event 1	Event 2
Columbus discovering America	Neil Armstrong landing on the Moon

   b Why do you think the writer has done this?

3 Imagine you had to give a brief radio report based on the key ideas in this article.

   List the key ideas and then write them up into a report to be read on the radio.

4 Explain the impact of the choice of language in each of the following quotations.

   a What does the phrase 'a global football competition' suggest about the space race?

   b What does the sentence 'enthusiasm for space exploration seemed to fizzle out' suggest about people's view of space travel?

5 Re-read paragraph 5. What effect do you think the writer wanted to achieve by asking this series of questions?

6 What is the effect of printing some words and phrases in a different colour?

7 How does the writer try to make the reader interested in this article? Your answer should include comments on:
   ● the way the writer tries to make the reader feel involved
   ● the choice of language to describe different events
   ● the use of pictures to make the article appealing
   ● any other features that make the article interesting.

Web texts

Text B is giving information about holidays in space; Text C is persuading you to visit the Kennedy Space Center.

8   Complete the table below, explaining some of the similarities and differences between these two texts.

Feature	Text B: NASA web page	Text C: Meet an Astronaut
Similarities in content		
Differences in content		
Similarities in purpose/ effect on the reader		
Differences in purpose/ effect on the reader		
Similarities in choice of style/use of language		
Differences in choice of style/use of language		
Similarities in structure/ presentation		
Differences in structure/ presentation		

Is space travel a good thing or is it waste of time and money?

9   Identify and list all the arguments **for** space travel and **against** space travel in this article.

10   Choose two of the FAQs and write a response to the arguments each one puts forward. You can use ideas and arguments from elsewhere in the material you have been given.

11   Look again at all the texts on pages 95–7.

   a   List the main arguments in favour of space travel.

   b   List the main arguments against space travel.

   c   Write a letter to a newspaper, summarising the arguments **either** for **or** against space travel and adding your own opinions.

5 Subject-specific language

You are learning:
- to plan writing and develop ideas to suit a specific audience.

Earlier in this unit you considered how ICT has influenced and changed language. Other groups in society also have their own vocabularies and forms of language. The review below is about a performance by the band Beirut. It is taken from the Glastonbury festival website.

Activity 1

1 Read the text and make a list of any subject-specific words that show that this article is a music review.

2 Underline any unfamiliar words in your list. First, guess their meaning using the context of the article. Then use a dictionary or the Internet to check their definitions.

Reviews
Stages
Other Areas & Venues
Blogs
Galleries
Performance
Out & About
Interviews
Media
gastONline

glastONline > Reviews > Stages

Beirut
Jazz World Stage
Sunday

New York meets New Mexico ensemble, Beirut, spilled onto the Jazz World stage early on Sunday evening with a mass of marching brass. The fanfare eventually subsided, allowing 20-year-old lead singer Zach Condon's indecipherable wail to emerge along with a couple of ukuleles and an accordion.

Glastonbury was about to be treated to a shambolically splendid dose of Balkan gypsy folk. Beirut are a new take on 'the next big thing' – think uplifting funeral marching band and you'll get the idea. And it seemed that the word had spread: a larger than usual crowd had made their way over to the Jazz World in anticipation of the band's Glastonbury debut.

Second track 'Brandenburg' drew a resounding cheer from an audience that seemed to have that 'I'm in the know about this undiscovered cool band' look. Rattling drums kept the march in time and the accordion, mini-guitars and violins created a brilliant blend of Romany Rock. And guess what? Not a gypsy in sight.

Substituting trumpet for voice on the chorus sections is a stroke of brilliance and enables the tormented young Zach to vent his post-teenage angst far more effectively. The songs have a 'real' feeling to them and when he mumbles, 'Some days, I feel all alone,' you believe it because the music has already told you.

Activity 2

1 As the popularity of the Glastonbury festival continues to grow, so does the variety of people who attend the festival. Think about who might be the intended audience(s) of this review and what the purposes of the review might be. Add your ideas to the list below.

Audience	Purpose
People who did not manage to get tickets to the festival	To encourage people's interest in future festivals
Commercial companies involved in the music/record world	

2 Which do you think would be most appropriate for the audiences and purposes you have identified – an informal or formal writing style? Give reasons for your answer.

Activity 3

Look at the features of a review text listed below. Copy out an example from the review on page 100 to illustrate each one. The first example is done for you.

- value judgements by the reviewer, e.g. *it's unusual, different and superbly entertaining*
- use of the third person
- use of specialist vocabulary
- vocabulary of description

- orientation (factual details of when, who, what, where)
- past tense to record a specific event
- present tense to comment on the quality of a product
- proper nouns (names of people, places, titles).

Activity 4

Now write your own review of a song that you like or dislike. Try to include as many features of a review text as you can.

Sharpen your skills Speech punctuation

Speech marks are used to mark the actual words that someone speaks (direct speech). They are also used to quote someone's written words. Look at the email extract below that describes a conversation about watching a live gig by the band Guillemots. Write out three sentences of direct speech that reflect the original conversation. An example is done for you.

I asked Ian what he thought of the Guillemots gig at the Cheltenham town hall which was part of the Jazz festival. I told him I thought it was totally amazing. There were some strange sounds but I said I couldn't believe they managed to play for so long without any music or formal plan. Ian couldn't stand it. He told me he thought it was a dreadful noise and he left after the first half hour.

Speak soon

Bob

- *'What did you think of the Guillemots gig at Cheltenham Town Hall?' asked Bob.*

6 Carrying out research

Television is one of the most popular and influential forms of communication. Debates still rage amongst parents, social commentators and the media about the pros and cons of TV's influence on children.

Activity 1

Read the article below and write a paragraph to summarise the author's viewpoint in your own words.

Explanation

ADHD **attention deficit hyperactivity disorder**

How TV is (quite literally) killing us

by Dr Aric Sigman, *Daily Mail* 1 October 2005

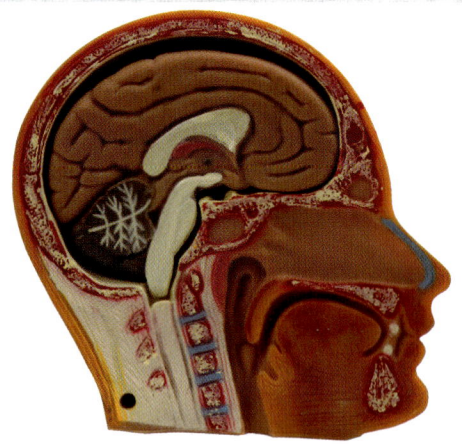

What, I wondered, would Baird make of TV now? What would he think of Jerry Springer's jeering mob? What would he make of television becoming more popular than shopping or going to the pub, church or library combined?

Or that more people would vote in a TV contest (*Pop Idol*) than for the Prime Minister and his entire party at the last election?

More pertinently, would he ever believe that his remarkable invention would come to represent one of the greatest dangers to the health of Britain and its social well-being at the dawn of the 21st century?

I've spent months poring over articles in journals ranging from *The Lancet* and *New England Journal of Medicine* to *Nature* and the *Journal of Neuroscience*.

The picture I formed was profoundly disturbing and amounts to what I believe to be the greatest health scandal of our time. I learned that viewing even moderate amounts of television:

* may damage brain cell development and function
* is the only adult pastime from the ages of 20 to 60 positively linked to developing Alzheimer's disease

- is a direct cause of obesity – a bigger factor even than eating junk food or taking too little exercise
- significantly increases the risk of Type 2 diabetes
- may biologically trigger premature puberty
- leads to a significantly elevated risk of sleep problems in adulthood, causing hormone changes which in turn increase body-fat production and appetite, damages the immune system and may lead to a greater vulnerability to cancer
- is a major independent cause of clinical depression (of which Britain has the highest rate in Europe).

These are not wild suppositions: they are based on hard, clinical evidence that has lain buried in academic journals.

For example, scientists at the University of Washington studied 2500 children and found a strong link between early television exposure and attention problems by age seven which was 'consistent with a diagnosis of ADHD'.

For every hour of television a child watches a day, they noted a nine per cent increase in attentional damage.

Equally shocking was the report in the medical journal *Pediatrics*, which studied the metabolic rates of 31 children while undertaking a variety of activities and found that when they watched TV, the children burned the equivalent of 211 calories fewer per day than if they did absolutely nothing.

In Bhutan – the last country on earth to introduce TV – I was appalled to discover that since the arrival of 46 cable channels, the country was experiencing its first serious crime wave. Greed, avarice and selfishness had replaced traditional values of peace and respect.

Bhutanese academics had conducted a study which showed how television was to blame for increasing crime, corruption and dramatically changing attitudes to relationships.

They were particularly appalled to discover that more than a third of parents now preferred to watch television than talk to their own children.

Consider the facts. By the age of 75, most of us will have spent more than twelve-and-a-half years of 24-hour days watching television. It has become the industrialised world's main activity,

taking up more of our time than any other single activity except work and sleep.

Children now spend more time watching a television screen than they spend in school. At this very moment, the average six-year-old will have already watched television for nearly one full year of their lives.

When other screen-based viewing, such as computer games, is included, the figure is far higher. Children aged 11 to 15 now spend 53 hours a week watching TV and computers – an increase of 40 per cent in a decade.

The health implications for our children are particularly worrying with the finding that television viewing among children under three seems to damage their future learning abilities – permanently.

"the average six-year-old will have already watched television for nearly one full year"

The statistics bear this out. Children who have televisions in their bedrooms at ages eight and nine score worst in school achievement tests. And a 26-year study, tracking children from birth, has just concluded 'television viewing in childhood and adolescence is associated with poor educational achievement by 26 years of age'.

Significant long-term damage occurs even at so-called 'modest levels' of viewing – between one and two hours a day.

Confronted with such evidence, I would argue that reducing our screen time must now be a health priority.

Ultimately, people will have to decide for themselves how much and what type of television they and their children watch – but they must now be made aware that there is a dark side to John Logie Baird's 'seeing by wireless' machine.

Activity 2

1 How does the writer suggest that his point of view has been scientifically proven to be correct – and that we should believe and agree with him? Use evidence from the text to support your answer.

2 a There are several points in the article about the negative effects of television. Does the writer mention any of its possible positive effects?

b Why do you think this is?

Activity 3

1 What do you think are the advantages of children watching television? Make a list of up to ten points then choose your best three. An example has been done for you.

> ● Children can learn information from factual programmes such as the news and documentaries.
>
> ●

2 Make and carry out a survey to assess:
- the amount of TV watched by members of your class
- the kinds of programmes they watch
- their opinions on the points that the article makes.

3 Record your research findings in an appropriate format such as a bar chart, pie chart or table.

TV Questionnaire

a) How much TV do you watch on average per week?
☐ none ☐ up to 5 hours
☐ up to 20 hours ☐ over 20 hours

b) What kinds of programmes do you watch?
☐ Soaps ☐ Documentaries
☐ Sport ☐ News
☐ Cookery ☐ Other

c) Do you think children should be banned from watching TV?
☐ Yes ☐ No

d) Do you think watching a lot of TV is harmful?
☐ Yes ☐ No

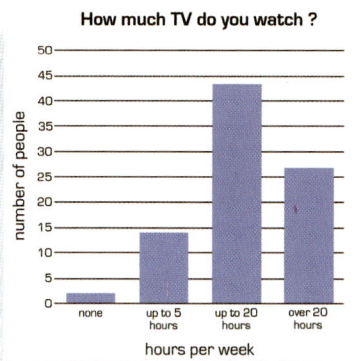

How much TV do you watch ?

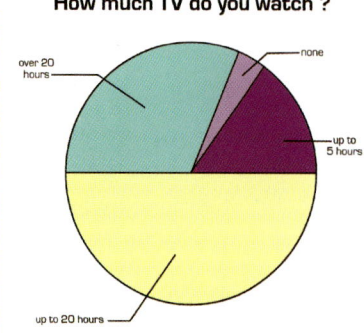

How much TV do you watch ?

How much TV do you watch per week ?	Number of people
none	2
up to 5 hours	13
up to 20 hours	43
over 20 hours	27

Assess your progress

FOR

I think children should be allowed TVs in their bedrooms.

AGAINST

I don't agree with children having TVs in their bedroom.

How confident are you about identifying arguments for and against? Make a copy of the table below and fill it in with two arguments for and two arguments against children having TVs in their bedroom. Try to fill in the table within 5 minutes, then identify your confidence level with your choices of argument by using the green, amber and red traffic lights next to your table.

not confident

quite confident

very confident

Points for TVs in children's bedrooms	Points against TVs in children's bedrooms

Sharpen your skills   Apostrophes for possession

Apostrophes are used to show that something belongs to or is connected with someone. The apostrophe should be positioned after the noun that defines that person, for example:

Andrew's pencil case.

The paragraph below is a student's description of her family's television-watching habits. Underline any errors in the use of apostrophes and write out the correct version.

Our familys television habits are quite varied. My sisters obsession is the soaps and because of this she probably watches about 9 hours of those per week, before you even start counting other programmes! My little brothers TV watching is much less. He is only 6 and my father limits his TV time. My parents watching habits are more difficult to comment on. My mother has the TV on in the kitchen a lot but isn't really watching it! My dads main love is his computer, but he watches about an hour of TV a night which is usually the news.

7 Presenting a balanced analysis

You are learning:
● to present a balanced analysis of an event or issue.

Some of us have strong points of view for or against a particular argument. However, there are many times in life where we need to make a compromise with people who have different views from our own.

Activity 1

Look back at the article on pages 102–103 and the feedback you gathered from members of your class in Activity 3 on page 104. Complete a table like the one below, listing as many relevant points as possible to summarise both sides of the argument.

For children watching TV	Against children watching TV

Activity 2

Let him watch what he wants! You try telling him to turn off his favourite programme. And it doesn't do him any harm!

He watches far too much rubbish and there are hundreds of other things he could be doing. I'm selling that stupid television!

What compromises could you suggest to these parents which both of them might agree with? Write down three suggestions.

Activity 3

Read this letter from a concerned mother.

Dear Agony Aunt,

My husband was brought up in a family where they watched no TV. Our child is now 3 years old and has not had TV which my husband and I agreed was the best way. However, I think this means I am having to care and play with him during all his waking hours and I'm exhausted without the break that many of my friends get when their child watches children's TV for an hour. I also wonder about the impact of this when he is older and at school. Can you give me your opinion about what I should do?

A concerned mother

Write three paragraphs of advice for the concerned mother, giving her a balanced outline of the issues and a viewpoint that would offer some compromise. You could use the following structure:

Paragraph 1: the negative side of children watching television.
Paragraph 2: the positive side of children watching television.
Paragraph 3: your suggestions for a compromise.

Sharpen your skills Paragraphs

A paragraph is a group of sentences about one main idea. For example, a report about school ICT facilities might be made up of the five paragraphs listed opposite.

Write three paragraphs about your television-watching habits. Then give each paragraph a title that summarises the main idea it contains.

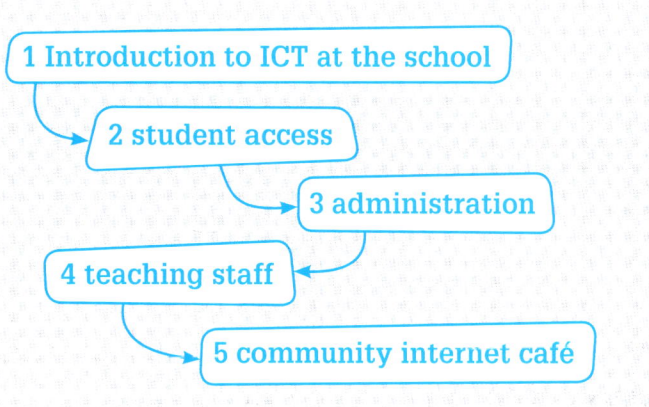

1 Introduction to ICT at the school
2 student access
3 administration
4 teaching staff
5 community internet café

Assessment task

Writing: Composition and conventions

TV Tantrum!

A newspaper is giving readers the opportunity to write a review of the programme or the type of programme they absolutely *loathe*!

This is the notice that appears in the paper:

Is there something you hate on television? Soap operas? Football? Reality shows? Makeover programmes?

We want readers' reviews of programmes or types of programme that make you want to hurl your TV through the window…

This is your chance to let off steam!

Your task

Write a review of a television programme you loathe in response to this newspaper notice.

Look again at the key features of a review text on page 101 to help you.

You will be assessed on:
- your selection of ideas and how you present them
- the range of sentences you use
- your choice of vocabulary and punctuation for effect.

Here are some phrases to help you:

Who thought it was a good idea to…?

Only a half-witted numbskull would…

It was the longest, dullest, most brain…

Anyone with any common sense knows…

I can't believe it was described as…

The presenter looked as though…

So, if you're reading this…

5 History of language

Objectives

In this unit you will:

Reading
- read signs and picture writing, explaining how they create effect and meaning
- use reading strategies to retrieve relevant information from texts.

Composition
- write a description in Middle English

Language
- understand the importance of using standard English when appropriate
- understand how and why to use different degrees of formality and informality
- develop your knowledge of spelling skills and strategies
- explain how linguistic concepts are related
- investigate spoken English from different regions and situations
- investigate texts from the past 1000 years to see how the English language has changed.

By the end of this unit you will:

- Listen to an interview, making notes as you listen in order to answer questions (Speaking and Listening: Listening and responding)
- Read and answer questions on two different texts about using slang (Reading: Reading for meaning)

Cross-curricular links

- **History**
  Cultural, ethnic and religious diversity; Change and continuity; Using evidence; The impact through time of the movement and settlement of diverse people to, from and within the British Isles.

1 Non-verbal communication

Scientists think that humans learnt to speak somewhere between 500,000 and 1.5 million years ago. Long before that, humans had the ability to communicate without words. This is called *non-verbal communication*. We still use non-verbal communication today.

Activity 1

1 How do you know when a dog is happy?

2 How do you know when a human being is happy?

3 Using only your body, and without using words, give the following messages:
   a I'm hungry.
   b I think we should both go over there.
   c You smell.
   d I disagree.

4 Think of three more messages to communicate to a partner. Can they guess them all?

Activity 2

What do you do if you want to communicate a message to someone who cannot see you? Today we send them a text, an email or a letter. But what would you have done 40,000 years ago? Cave paintings were one way in which our ancestors communicated with each other.

This is a cave painting from Lascaux in south-western France, showing a man and a bison. What do you think the artist is trying to say to whoever looks at it?

Activity 3

As far as we know, the first kind of writing was picture writing. Between 2000 and 5000 years ago, the Ancient Egyptians communicated using hieroglyphics: pictures that represented words. For example, the picture ⊙ was used to mean 'sun'. Pictures also came to represent ideas as well as things. The same symbol came to mean *light*, *warmth*, *day* or *time*.

1   We still use pictures and images to communicate today.
   a   Look at these symbols.

   b   Make a copy of the table below and use it to explore what the symbols mean and how they **create** their meaning. The first one has been started to help you:

	What do you see?	What does this suggest?
Symbol A	Lions Shield	The lions suggest the team is strong. The shield suggests...
Symbol B		
Symbol C		

   c   Think of three more symbols. Swap with a partner to write about **what** they mean and **how** they create their meaning.
   d   We noticed above that lions can be a symbol of strength. What could you use the images on the right to symbolise?

Activity 4

1   Look at these signs. They both mean the same thing. Why is one more effective than the other?

2   Design a sign to communicate one of the following messages without using any letters or words:
   a   Beware of the dog!
   b   No eating or drinking
   c   Silence, please.

2 Fifteen centuries of change

You are learning:
- to recognise how language has changed over time.

The language that we speak, write and read is changing all the time. Language has been changing since the first words were spoken, written and read.

Activity 1

These five texts were all written during the last 1500 years. All were written in Great Britain, using the language spoken at that time. If you were going to put these texts in the order in which they were written, what clues would you use to work out the correct order?

Text 1

A good wif was ther of biside Bathe,
But she was somdel deef, and that was scathe.
Of clooth-makyng she hadde swich an haunt
She passed hem of Ypres and of Gaunt.
In al the parisshe wif ne was ther noon
That to the offrynge bifore hire sholde goon;
And if ther dide, certeyn so wrooth was she
That she was out of alle charitee.

Text 2

So things were ticking along quite nicely. In fact, I'd say that good stuff had been happening pretty solidly for about six months.

* For example: Mum got rid of Steve, her rubbish boyfriend.

* For example: Mrs Gillett, my art and design teacher, took me to one side after a lesson and asked whether I'd thought of doing art at art college.

* For example: I'd learned two new skating tricks, suddenly, after weeks of making an idiot of myself in public.

Text 3

London. Michaelmas term lately over, and the Lord Chancellor sitting in Lincoln's Inn Hall. Implacable November weather. As much mud in the streets as if the waters had but newly retired from the face of the earth, and it would not be wonderful to meet a Megalosaurus, forty feet long or so, waddling like an elephantine lizard up Holborn Hill. Smoke lowering down from chimney-pots, making a soft black drizzle, with flakes of soot in it as big as full-grown snowflakes—gone into mourning, one might imagine, for the death of the sun. Dogs, undistinguishable in mire. Horses, scarcely better; splashed to their very blinkers.

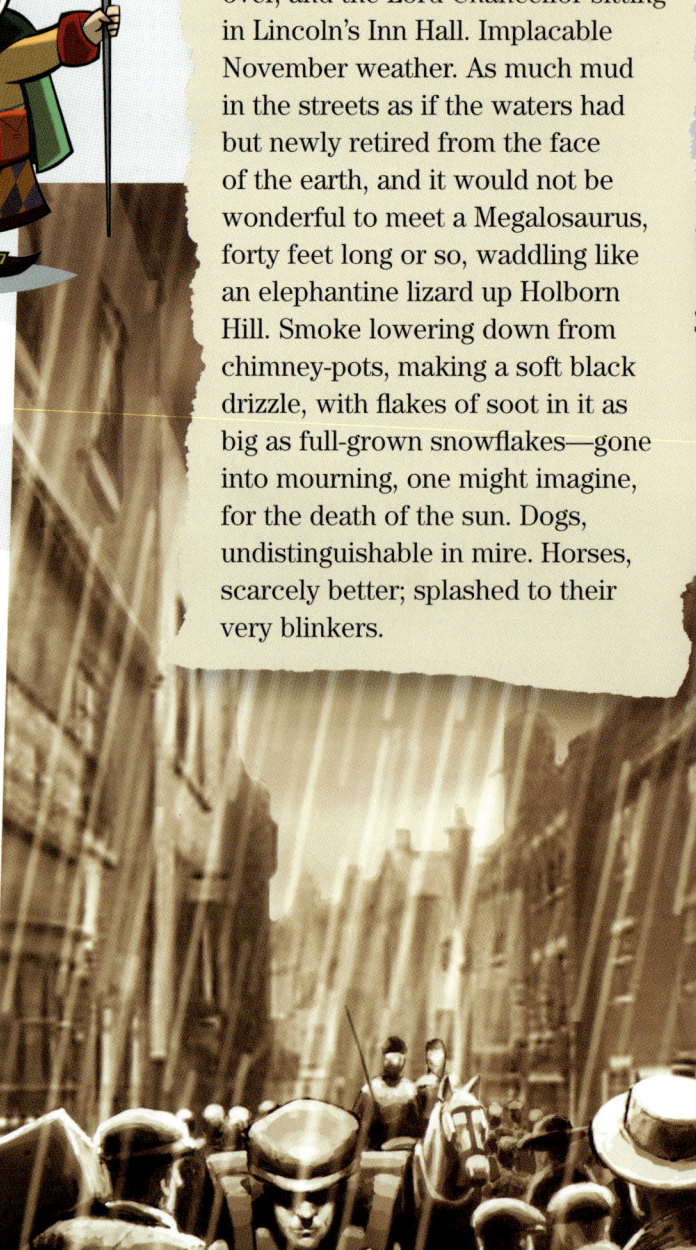

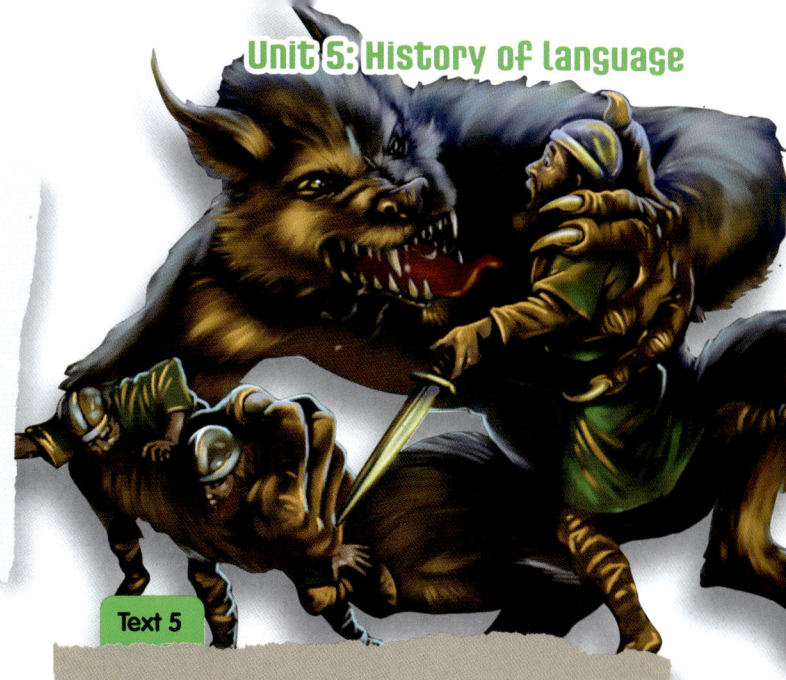

Text 4

Shall I compare thee to a Summer's day?
Thou art more lovely and more temperate:
Rough winds do shake the darling buds of May,
And Summer's lease hath all too short a date:
Sometimes too hot the eye of heaven shines,
And often is his gold complexion dimmed,
And every fair from fair sometime declines,
By chance, or nature's changing course untrimmed.

Text 5

...þryðswyð beheold
mæg Higelaces,   hu se manscaða
under færgripum   gefaran wolde.
Ne þæt se aglæca   yldan þohte,
ac he gefeng hraðe   forman siðe
slæpendne rinc,   slat unwearnum,

Dates
between 700 and 1000
around 1380
around 1600
1853
2007

Activity 2

1   Which text was written when? Try to match the texts to the dates.

2   How did you work it out? Here are some clues you might have used. Tick the ones you used, giving an example from one or more of the five texts.

Clue	Used ✓	Example
How easy the text was to understand		
What the writer was writing about		
The words the writer used		

Assess your progress

This table shows you how to get better at recognising the ways in which language changes. How well are you doing?

Level 4	Level 5	Level 6
I can say which texts are old and which are more recent	I can explain the clues I used to work out the order in which the texts were written and give examples	I can comment on some of the ways in which English has changed in the last 1500 years

3 Invaders

You are learning:

● to explore how Latin and Greek have contributed to the English language.

Great Britain has been invaded four times in its history.

The original Britons (the Celts), and their language (Celtic), survived only in the furthest corners of Great Britain. In Wales, Scotland, Ireland, Cornwall and the Isle of Man, versions of Celtic are still spoken – and have been since long before the Roman invasion 2000 years ago.

2 In the 5th and 6th centuries the Angles, Saxons and Jutes came to Britain from what is now Germany and Denmark.

3 In the 7th and 8th centuries the Vikings invaded from what is now Scandinavia.

1 In AD 43 the Romans invaded.

4 In 1066, William the Conqueror and the Normans invaded Britain from northern France.

3 Yorkshire/ Lancashire

1 Kent

2 Sussex   **4 Hastings**

Activity 1

The Romans spoke a language called Latin.

An etymological dictionary shows the origins of words. In this extract from an etymological dictionary, English words that come from Latin are indicated by **L.**

Explanation

> **etymology** the history of a word

1   How many words of Latin origin can you spot?

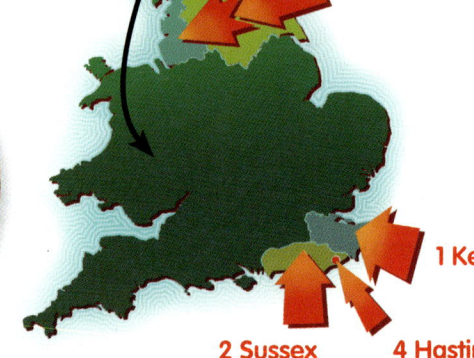

flora the plant life of a region or epoch, from L. *Flora* Roman goddess of flowers, from *flos* flower.

florescence from L. *florescentem* 'blooming,'.

floret 1583, from *florete*, 'flower,' from L. *flora*

florid 'strikingly beautiful,' from *floride* 'flourishing,' from L. *floridus* 'flowery, blooming,' from *flos* 'flower' (see *flora*).

florin from *florin, fiorino, fiore* 'flower,' from L. *florem* 'flower' (see *flora*).

florist 1623, formed on analogy of *fleuriste*, from L. *floris, flos* 'flower.'

floss (n.) 'rough silk,' 1759, from *floche* 'tuft of wool,' from *floc*, from L. *floccus* 'tuft of wool.'

flotilla 1711, 'a small fleet,' from *flotilla, flota* 'float,' from *flotar* 'to float,' (see *float*).

flotsam 1607, from Anglo-Fr. *floteson, flotaison* 'a floating,' from *floter* 'to float'.

Activity 2

The Romans left Britain in the fifth century, but the lasting influence of Latin began with the arrival of Christianity. This was because Latin was the language of the Church and of teaching and learning. During the sixteenth and seventeenth centuries, Ancient Greek and Ancient Roman culture had a huge influence on our literature, law, science and many other areas of learning – including language.

1   Many English words begin with Greek or Latin prefixes, or end with Greek or Latin suffixes. How many words can you think of that start or end with the prefixes and suffixes listed in the table below?

prefixes	meaning	suffixes	meaning
micro- (Greek)	small	-gon (Greek)	angle
multi- (Latin)	many	-phobia (Greek)	horror
sub- (Latin)	under, less than	-ology (Greek)	study
tele- (Greek)	far off, distant	-cide (Latin)	kill

Sharpen your skills Possessive pronouns

Possessive pronouns replace a noun, showing who something belongs to – who possesses it.

Possessive pronouns **never** have apostrophes – but it is sometimes easy to confuse them with contractions that do use apostrophes.

It's time for the dog to eat its food.

A contraction of *it is*. The apostrophe shows that a letter has been missed out.

A possessive pronoun. The food belongs to the dog.

Possessive pronouns
mine
yours
his
hers
its
ours
theirs

1   Pick out the possessive pronouns in these sentences:
   a   It's mine. Where's yours?
   b   My budgie's happy when it's in its cage.
   c   There's no way of knowing which is theirs.

2   a   Write three sentences using all of these words correctly at least once:
       it's   its   there's   theirs
   b   Underline all the possessive pronouns in your sentences.
   c   Circle any contractions you have used.

4 Investigating Old English

You are learning:

- to explore the relationship between Modern English and Old English.

The English language has been through four main stages in the last 1500 years. Old English was the first of these stages. It developed from the languages of the Anglo-Saxons and the Vikings. One of the most important and well-known texts that has survived from that time is *Beowulf*, a long poem that tells the story of a heroic warrior, Beowulf, kinsman of King Higelac, and his battle to protect his people from a terrible monster called Grendel.

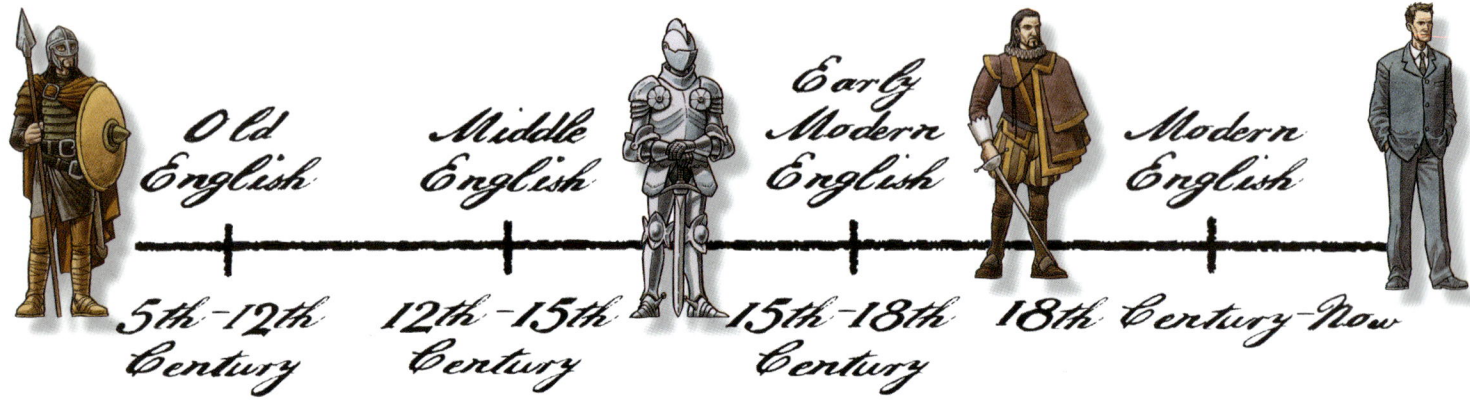

Old English — 5th–12th Century

Middle English — 12th–15th Century

Early Modern English — 15th–18th Century

Modern English — 18th Century–Now

Activity 1

In this extract, Grendel has come to King Higelac's hall where all the warriors are sleeping. The creature thinks he will eat well, feasting on their flesh. He grabs and devours one of the sleeping warriors – but Beowulf is awake and waiting for him.

1   Read the Old English text aloud. It has some letters and sounds you will not recognise:

> æ is pronounced as a short 'a', as in *cat*
> þ and ð are pronounced 'th' as in *thing* or *brother*

... he gefeng hraðe   forman siðe
he (Grendel) grabbed quickly first time
slæpendne rinc, slat unwearnum,
sleeping warrior wounded suddenly
bat banlocan, blod edrum dranc,
bit muscle   blood vein drank
synsnædum swealh; sona hæfde
chunks swallowed; soon had
unlyfigendes eal gefeormod,
eaten   all the dead man
fet ond folma. Forð near ætstop,
foot and hand. Onwards nearer stepped
nam þa mid handa   higeþihtigne
seized then with hand courageous
rinc on ræste,   ræhte ongean
warrior on bed reached towards

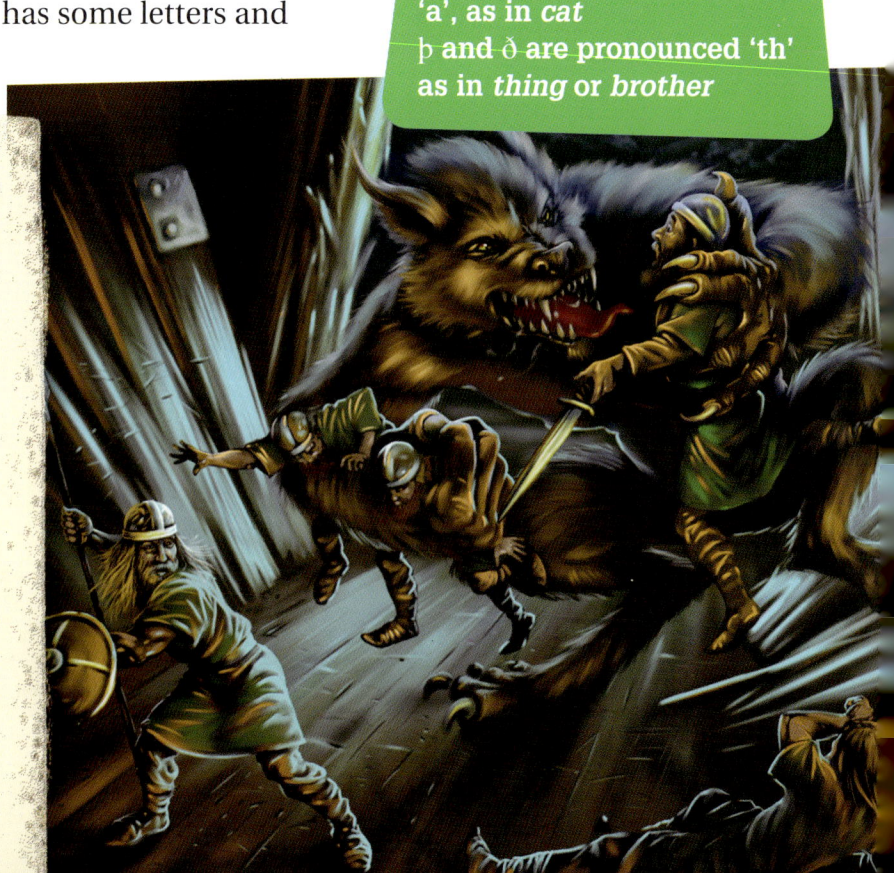

feond mid folme; he onfeng hraþe
fiend with hand   he took hold of quickly
inwitþancum   ond wið earm gesæt.
with evil intent and with arm bent.
Sona þæt onfunde   fyrena hyrde
Soon that discovered evil guardian
þæt he ne mette middangeardes,
that he not met   the world
eorþan sceata,   on elran men
Earth's surface on other men
mundgripe maran.
a mightier handgrasp.

2 a Translate a few lines into modern English, using the
translation beneath the Old English to help you. You may
need to add some extra words to help it make sense.

   b What do you notice about the order in which the words are
written in Old English?

3 a Are there any words in Old English that are similar to modern
English? It could be that they sound similar or remind you of
another modern word with the same meaning. Divide them
into categories using a table like the one below.

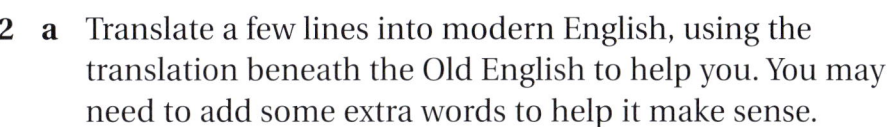

Nouns, verbs, adverbs and adjectives	Other words

   b What do you notice about the kind of words that have
survived in Modern English?

   c If only a few Old English words are still used today, which
languages do you think all our other words have come from?

Activity 2

1 a When the Vikings invaded in the seventh and eigth centuries
they brought the influence of their language – Old Norse. This
did not replace the Anglo-Saxons' language but added to it.
English was beginning to develop a large and rich vocabulary.
Look at these words and their origins:

   b Put the words in matching pairs. Write a sentence for each
pair in which the words can be swapped without changing
the overall meaning. For example:
My uncle rears/raises pigs on his farm.

Anglo-Saxon	Old Norse
craft	anger
rear	ill
sick	raise
wrath	skill

5 Middle English

You are learning:
● to explore Middle English.

In 1066 the Normans invaded Britain. William the Conqueror defeated King Harold at the Battle of Hastings, and French became the language of the ruling classes.

Activity 1

Three hundred years after 1066, English became the language of Great Britain again. But with the influence of French, it had developed from Old English into what is now called Middle English.

Geoffrey Chaucer's poem *The Canterbury Tales* was written in Middle English at the end of the fourteenth century. It is one of the first English texts about real people and their everyday lives. It is about a group of pilgrims travelling to Canterbury, telling stories to pass the time. This extract is from his description of one pilgrim: the Wife of Bath.

A good wif was ther of biside Bathe,
But she was somdel deef, and that was scathe.
...
Hir coverchiefs ful fyne weren of ground;
I dorste swere they weyeden ten pound
That on a sonday weren upon hir heed.
Hir hosen weren of fyn scarlet reed,
Ful streite yteyd, and shoes ful moyste and newe.
Boold was hir face, and fair, and reed of hewe.
She was a worthy womman al hir lyve:
Housbondes at chirche dore she hadde fyve,
Withouten oother compaignye in youthe, –
But therof nedeth nat to speke as nowthe...
Gat-tothed was she, soothly for to seye.
Upon an amblere esily she sat,
Ywympled wel, and on hir heed an hat
As brood as is a bokeler or a targe;
A foot-mantel aboute hir hipes large,
And on hir feet a paire of spores sharpe.
In felaweshipe wel koude she laughe and carpe.
Of remedies of love she knew per chaunce,
For she koude of that art the olde daunce.

somdel: somewhat, rather
scathe: a pity
ground: texture

hosen: stockings
streite yteyd: tightly fastened
of hewe: in colour

withouten: not counting
as nowthe: right now
gat-tothed: gap-toothed
soothly: truthfully
amblere: pacing horse
ywympled wel: wearing a large wimple
bokeler/targe: small shields
foot-mantel: over-skirt

carpe: chatter
per chaunce: by chance
koude: knew

1   Try reading the extract aloud. What do you notice about Middle English? Are there any words you recognise?

2   Using the notes and your knowledge of modern English to help you, either write a translation in Modern English or draw a picture of the Wife of Bath, including all the details Chaucer gives.

Activity 2

Some of the words Chaucer uses have survived without any change.
Other words have changed, and some words are not used at all in Modern
English. Find five of each and write them in a table like the one below.

Words that have survived	Words that have changed	Words we do not use at all
good	wif	somdel

Activity 3

1   You are going to write a description of a person in Middle English.
    First, collect some Middle English vocabulary from the extract on
    page 118. Find as many words as you can to complete this table:

Parts of the body	Clothing	Adjectives
heed	hosen	reed

2   Choose a person to write your description about.

3   Write your description. Aim to write about 10–15 lines, using as
    much Middle English as you can. If you don't know the Middle
    English word, use the Modern English word. **Don't** make it up!

Assess your progress

Use this table to decide the level you are working at.

Level 4	Level 5	Level 6
• I can identify the meaning of some Middle English words • I used one or two Middle English words in my writing	• I can understand most of the Middle English text • I used some Middle English vocabulary in my writing	• I am confident in my understanding of the Middle English text • I used a wide range of Middle English vocabulary in my writing

Sharpen your skills — Personal pronouns

Personal pronouns are used to stand for nouns: *I, you, he, she, it, we, they*. Read the story below. Which nouns would you replace with pronouns?

Helen and Roger went to the cinema together.
'What film does Helen want to see?' asked Roger.
'Helen would like to see the romantic film,' said Helen.
'Roger and Helen could go for a meal instead,' Roger suggested.
'There is a Chinese restaurant on the High Street. The Chinese restaurant has a special offer on at the moment,' said Helen.
Roger and Helen went to the restaurant.

6 Early Modern English

You are learning:
- to explore the development of Early Modern English through the language of Shakespeare.

At the end of the fifteenth century, two things happened which helped change the English language and make it much more recognisable as Modern English:
- the printing press was invented, which meant that more people had access to a wider variety of books
- the Tudor dynasty came to the throne, bringing wealth, stability and more trade. People were travelling, trading and communicating across the nation more than ever before.

Activity 1

Shakespeare wrote in Early Modern English between 1592 and 1613. It has been estimated that, in all his writing, he used a total of around 20,000 different words and was the first person to use 1700 of them! Below are just a few of them, with an explanation of how Shakespeare created them.

eventful	noun + **ful** = adjective to describe a time full of events
quarrelsome	noun + **some** = adjective to describe one who quarrels a lot
stealthy	noun + **y** = adjective to describe someone who has stealth
droplet	noun + **let** = a smaller drop
moonbeam	two nouns joined together to make a new noun
uncomfortable, unreal	**un** + adjective = the opposite
well-behaved, well-read	**well-** + verb = someone who behaves well, reads a lot
to gossip	a *gossip* was a close friend. Shakespeare was the first to use the noun as a verb: something you do with your close friends

1 Copy this table of nouns, verbs and adjectives, and add three words to each column.

Nouns	Verbs	Adjectives
dog	to joke	beautiful
party	to run	stupid
nose		

2 You can use these words to make new words, just like Shakespeare did. For example, you could say that:
- Someone with a good sense of humour is *well-joked*.
- A park in which there are lots of people walking their dogs is *dogful*.
- A week in which you go to a lot of parties is *partysome*.

Using the words from your completed table, invent five new words. For each one, write a sentence explaining what it means and how to use it.

3 Shakespeare wasn't perfect. He invented a lot of words that never caught on. Can you guess what these three might mean?
smilets   mistempered   rubious

Activity 2

English has changed since Shakespeare was writing, so it can be difficult to understand him. There are some simple rules that can help:

A quick guide to Early Modern English	
thee	you
thou	you
thy	your
thine	yours
hast	have
art	are
shalt	shall
doth	does
dost	do

Rule 1: personal pronouns

Thee and *thou* both mean 'you', **but**:
- *Thou* is the 'you' who loves (the subject of the verb).
- *Thee* is the 'you' who is being loved (the object).

Rule 2: verbs

- In the second person – you – the verb ends in -st: *lovest*.
- In the third person – he, she or it – the verb ends in -th: *loveth*.

Note: our verbs still do something a bit like this. In the third person we usually add an 's' to the verb: you love her, she love<u>s</u> you.

1 Without speaking, start a written conversation with a partner. Stop when you have written three lines each. Now try translating it into Early Modern English. It might start like this:

> What are you doing after school?
> What art thou doing after school?

Assess your progress

Continue your conversation on paper without speaking – but this time, write in Early Modern English from the start.

Every time your partner writes a line, award a point. If you spot a mistake in your partner's Early Modern English, take a point away. How many points canst thou make in five minutes?

Sharpen your skills Parts of a sentence

1 Read this sentence:

The dog bit the man.

The dog did the biting: <u>The dog</u> is the subject of the sentence.

Biting is the thing that happened: <u>bit</u> is the verb in the sentence.

The man was the thing that was bitten: <u>the man</u> is the object of the sentence.

2 Label these sentences, showing which word or phrase is the subject, the verb and the object:
   a The man bit the dog.
   b I cleaned the windows.
   c You know the answer.

7 Modern English

You are learning:
- to understand how other cultures and new inventions have contributed to the modern English language.

In the seventeenth and eighteenth centuries, Britain was trading with (and taking over) more and more countries, building its wealth and its empire. This not only meant that English was used in more and more countries, but also that English began to borrow words from other languages. It has been estimated that English now has loan words from over 140 languages.

Activity 1

A lot of the words English has borrowed from other languages are to describe things that English speakers had not seen until they went abroad. We strongly associate these words with the country we borrowed them from.

Explanation

> **loan word** a word that one language adopts from another language, for example *café* comes from French

1   **a**   Can you match each of the words in the table below to its original language?
b   For each word, write a short explanation of how you worked out the answer.

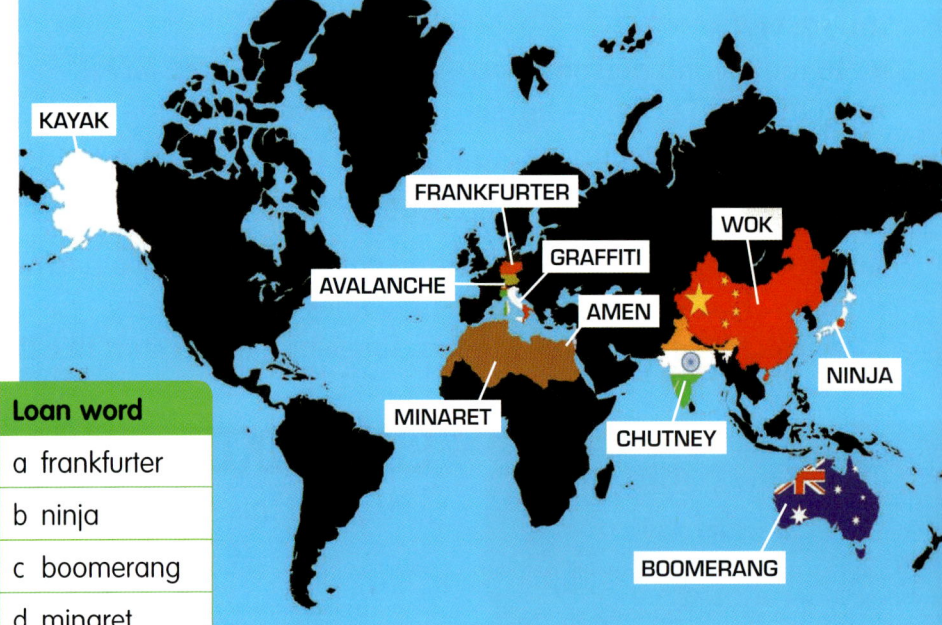

Language	Spoken in	Loan word
1 Cantonese	China	a frankfurter
2 Dharuk	Australia	b ninja
3 Hebrew	Israel	c boomerang
4 Inuit	Alaska	d minaret
5 Italian	Italy	e chutney
6 Japanese	Japan	f wok
7 Romanche	Switzerland	g kayak
8 German	Germany	h avalanche
9 Hindu	India	i amen
10 Arabic	Middle East, North Africa	j graffiti

2   The original, or literal, meaning of Frankfurter is *from Frankfurt*. Can you match the other loan words in question 1 to their original meanings from the list on the right?

scribbling	lamp, lighthouse	stealth
curved	pan	to taste
descent	small skin boat	truth

Activity 2

You've thought of a fantastic new invention. But what are you going to call it? This is the problem that inventors of fantastic new inventions have always faced: you need to invent a new word to go with it.

Duke of Wellington

Some inventors gave their own name to their creation or idea. Can you work out what these people invented?

- Lazslo Biro
- Louise Braille
- Robert Bunsen
- Samuel Morse
- Earl of Sandwich
- Rudolf Diesel
- Ferdinand von Zeppelin

Ernö Rubik

Activity 3

Technology has changed at a very fast pace in the last fifty years – and so has the language we use to talk about it. Thirty years ago, the word 'Internet' did not exist. Fifty years ago, a mouse was just a small rodent.

1   Can you think of any other words from the world of information technology which have either:
- changed their meaning *or*
- been invented?

Write them in a table like the one below.

New words	Words that have changed their meaning
Internet	Mouse

2   Choose three of the words from your table. For each one, write a sentence explaining why you think the word suits its meaning.

Sharpen your skills Negatives

In the English language, two negatives used together make a positive.

Make three tables like the one on the right to explain the true meaning of these three sentences.

When you say	He's not doing nothing tonight.
It's the opposite of	He's doing nothing tonight.
So it means	He will be busy tonight.

1   He's not never going to say sorry.

2   You're not going nowhere with him.

3   I don't know no-one here.

8 Comparing modern languages

You are learning:

● to recognise some of the connections between Modern English, German and French.

Lots of English words have their origins in Old German and French, brought to Britain by the Angles and Saxons and the Normans. So you may not be surprised that there are still a lot of similarities between English, German and French.

Activity 1

Many German words are related to English words, with just a few changes in spelling. Look at these spelling patterns:

● *pf*, *ff* and *f* in German sometimes change to *p* in English
● *ch* and *ck* in German sometimes change to *k* in English
● *sch* in German sometimes changes to *ch* or *sh* or *s* in English.

1 Can you work out what these German words mean?

Apfel   Pfeife   Storch   Fisch

Pfeffer   Milch   Scharf   Schimpanse

Activity 2

Some French words are even more recognisable to English speakers. Look at this menu. Can you work out what will be served – and when you might be eating it?

Dîner

Soupe aux tomates

Boeuf et carottes
Porc et brocolis

Bananes en sauce au caramel

Jus
Limonade
Vin

Assess your progress

1 Using a dictionary or the Internet, find out the origins of the words below. Are they from Latin, French or Anglo-Saxon? Or are they a loan word, a new word, or a word that has changed its meaning?

● avatar
● biscuit
● calendar
● data
● ebony
● Friday
● geyser
● hack
● inbox
● jungle

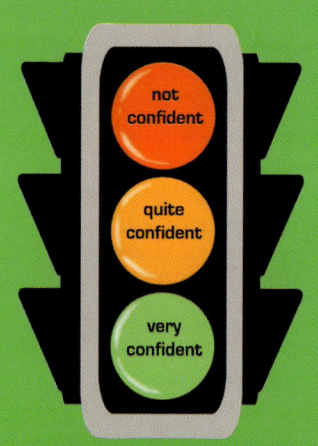

not confident

quite confident

very confident

2 Use the traffic lights to show how confident are you in identifying the origins of words.

Assessment task

Speaking and Listening: Listening and responding

A chat with John Simpson

Your task

Listen to the following 'chat' with John Simpson, who has been the Chief Editor of the *Oxford English Dictionary* (*OED*) since 1993. Make notes while you listen.

1 Use your notes to post a comment to John Simpson, explaining:
   a what you found interesting about the interview
   b what further questions you would like to ask him.

   Your comment needs to show how well you have listened to the interview.

Anu Garg (Moderator)
The topic of discussion is 'The World of Words: *OED*'.

Cathy Vickio – USA
Can a word be nominated for inclusion?

John Simpson (Guest Speaker)
Yes, but that doesn't necessarily get it in! On the *OED* we're looking for documentary evidence of a word's currency over say five years at least. We have readers and contributors throughout the world who provide examples … for us, and the editorial staff then work through the online and card files establishing which terms are well enough attested to be considered.

Bingley – Indonesia
Would you accept spoken evidence, such as TV or radio interviews?

John Simpson (Guest Speaker)
We do cite TV and radio material if we can obtain an official transcript. It's the same with films. And often we can. I think the first example of 'magic' in the *OED* as an exclamation comes from a film script which we obtained through the copyright holders. We 'read' scripts and song lyrics too – there's a lot that is actually published...

Languid – USA
Do you track words that become obsolete?

John Simpson (Guest Speaker)
The *OED* tracks all words – in Britain, America, Australia, etc. – wherever English is spoken, and at whatever level (formal, informal, etc.), and through time. So yes, tracking when a term becomes obsolete is as important to us as finding when a word originates.

Sierray – USA
I presume that words are dropped from the dictionary as they go out of use as well as added. Do you have any idea what the ratio is of dropped words to added words?

John Simpson (Guest Speaker)
No, the full *OED* is a cumulative dictionary. We don't drop words or meanings. We're covering English through the ages, and a meaning that flourished for a quarter of a century back in the 1500s is as important for us (maybe more so) than the latest computer jargon. So there isn't a ratio!

Ilana Wartenberg – Israel
How do you confront the surge of technical jargon, mostly related to the computer world, such that new words are constantly 'born'?

John Simpson (Guest Speaker)
We have a system of monitoring language through our 'reading programme'. We 'read' technical handbooks, scientific periodicals, popular magazines – on each subject. If we have amassed enough evidence – whether a term is technical or general – it can qualify for the *OED*.

Elaine Meil – USA
During what period were the most words added?

John Simpson (Guest Speaker)
…added to the language or added to the Dictionary? The former is the more interesting. Probably the greatest (relative) period of expansion was at the end of the sixteenth century. … It keeps on going upwards after that, but not at such a significant pace until the late nineteenth and early twentieth century. And I think things are shifting quite fast today too.

9 Language today

You are learning:
- to explore language change and formality.

The English language has been changing since the moment it began – and it's still changing. Why? It's because the world we talk and write about changes every day.

Activity 1

One example of language that changes very quickly is slang. Look at this graph showing how slang words meaning 'good' have come in and gone out of fashion over the last fifty years. How many of them have you used? Perhaps your parents will recognise some of the others?

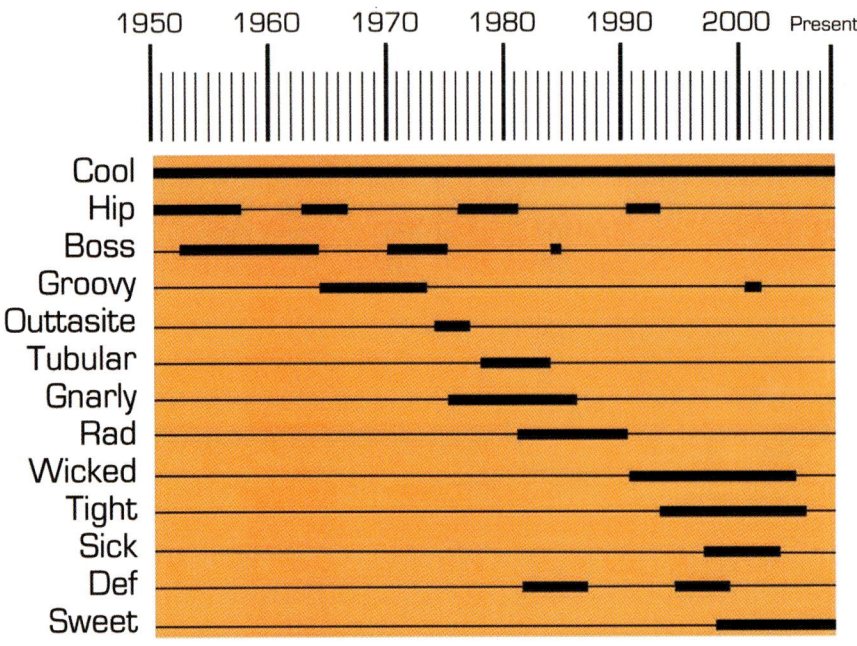

1 Which word has remained popular for the longest time?

2 Which word was popular for the shortest time?

3 Are there any other words you have ever used to show you like something? Are there any slang words you have ever used to show the opposite: that you dislike something? Record them in a table like this:

Approval	Disapproval

4 Which of these words are in fashion at the moment? Which are out of fashion? Write 'in' or 'out' next to each one.

5 What would happen if you used an old-fashioned slang word with your friends? Read the text in the speech bubble on the right. If you said this to your friends what would be their reply?

6 Why do you think people use slang? How would you feel if your teacher or your parents started using the same slang that you use? Would you carry on using it? Why?

7 Write a definition of the word 'slang'.

Listen to this tune. It's so groovy! Tubular!

Activity 2

A major change that has happened recently is text-messaging. It uses abbreviations to squeeze as much information as possible into the 160 characters available in each message.

1 Write a list of five or more words or phrases in text language.

2 Text-messaging uses lots of different methods of abbreviation. Write an explanation of the ones you have used. For example:

> Sometimes numbers are used to represent words or syllables: '2' instead of 'to'.

Activity 3

English has lots of words with similar meanings. This is because some come from Latin, some from French and some from Anglo-Saxon. With so many words, it's important to choose the right ones. Sometimes this depends on how formal or informal your language needs to be.

1 Look at these different ways of showing whether you approve or disapprove of something. Rank each column in order, with the first word or phrase being the most formal and the last being the most informal.

	Anglo-Saxon origin	Slang	Latin origin	Text language	French origin
Approval	That's good!	Cool!	Magnificent	QL!	How pleasing!
Disapproval	That's bad!	That stinks!	It's atrocious!	PU!	How terrible!

2 a Can you see any connection between the origin of the words and how formal or informal they are?
  b Think of a situation when text language would **not** be appropriate.
  c Think of a situation when words of Latin origin would **not** be appropriate.

Sharpen your skills Adverbs

Adverbs add information to verbs. They tell us how, when or where something happens or is done. How did he run? He ran *quickly*. When did he run? He ran *yesterday*. Where did he stop? He stopped *there*.

1 Fill the blanks on the right with adverbs.

2 Lots of adverbs end in -*ly*, but not all of them. And not all words that end in -*ly* are adverbs. By putting these words into a sentence, work out which ones are adverbs and which are not.

She screamed _____ . It was walking _____ towards her. She _____ began to run but she was breathing so _____ she could not escape.

- lovely
- lonely
- well
- quickly
- sometimes
- ugly
- often
- fast
- silly

10 Dialects

You are learning:
- to explore the different dialects of English.

Everywhere that English is spoken today, it is slightly different. There are different words for the same things and different rules for how words are organised into sentences. These different varieties are called dialects.

Explanation

dialects different versions of a language, spoken by people in different regions or areas

Activity 1

1   American English, spoken in the United States, uses lots of different words compared with the language spoken in Great Britain. Translate these American English words into British English.

American English		Definition	British English	
chips		a crunchy potato snack, often flavoured – cheese and onion, for example		
jelly		a spread made from fruit, often spread on toast		
pants		clothing to cover your legs		
sidewalk		area for walking on beside a road		
sneakers		shoes worn for sport		

2   **a**   Look again at the American English words. Do any of them mean something different in British English?

   b   What does this suggest about the different words in English dialects?

Activity 2

Standard English is another English dialect. It is the dialect used in formal speaking and writing. Sometimes people think of it as correct or proper English, or the 'Queen's English'. It is just another dialect which is appropriate on some occasions and in some situations.

Look at these examples from different dialects.

Standard English	Northern Irish English	Geordie	Brummie
baby	sprog	bairn	babby
friend	mucker	marra	skip
excellent	sound	champion	bostin

1   Which words do you use to mean *baby*, *friend* and *excellent* in the area where you live?

2   Do you think it is important for all students to learn to write and speak in standard English as well as their own dialect? Why?

Activity 3

Dialects don't just have their own words for different things – they also have different rules. Read this extract from a story about Anansi the spider, written in Caribbean dialect.

Anansi and Bredda Lion

Bredda Lion had a new bad habit. Every time he ate and went to sleep at night, he would belch really loud and wake up the rest of the village.

Anansi loved to sleep. Since Lion had developed this habit he has not gotten one night's sleep. Last night was the worst. He visited Bredda Rabbit and Bredda Snake to see how they were holding up.

'Bredda Rabbit, how yuh doing man?' asked Anansi, as he approached Bredda Rabbit outside his home.

'Mi doing just fine,' replied Bredda Rabbit.

'Yuh getting any sleep since Lion start dem big belchin?' asked Bredda Anansi.

'Yeah man, nuff sleep since mi buy dem ear muffs whey Bredda Snake tell me bout down a shop,' he replied.

'Ear muffs!' Anansi exclamated.

'Yes dem block out every sound, whey yuh nuh go buy some?' Bredda Rabbit explained.

1 **a** Write down any words you can find in the story that are from the Caribbean dialect.
   b What do you think they mean?

2 Look at these two sentences taken from the story:
   a Translate them into standard English.
   b What do you notice about the underlined verbs?

- Yuh getting any sleep since Lion <u>start</u> dem big belchin?
- Yeah man, nuff sleep since mi <u>buy</u> dem ear muffs

3 Look at these two phrases taken from the story:
   a Translate them into standard English
   b Which words are missing from the phrases?

- How yuh doing man?
- Mi doing just fine

4 Using your answers to questions 1, 2, and 3, write a short guide to the language and rules of Caribbean English.

Assess your progress

The most important thing in choosing the language you use is to think about the situation you are in and the method you are using to communicate. Which of these is appropriate for these purposes and audiences?

Language	Method	Purpose and audience
standard English	letter	applying for a job
dialect English	email	asking a friend a question
slang	text	asking a parent a favour
text language	conversation	explaining something to a teacher

Assessment task

Reading: Reading for meaning

Understanding slang

Your task

Read the two texts about using slang and answer the questions that follow.

Text 1

Academic text

Students are increasingly using text speak in exams and essays. Lecturer Adam Fox cdnt bleve wot he was cing

Wednesday March 17, 2004
Guardian Unlimited

Presumably I am not the only one to have received exam scripts written partly in text message English? It is a trend that we in our department have noticed quietly growing over the last two or three years.

Students writing quickly, particularly towards the end of an exam, will descend into the abbreviated jargon they use many times a day in communicating with their friends. I confess to never having sent a text message (I only acquired a mobile phone earlier this year): I suppose I must be one of the few people left in the country, under the age of 70, who hasn't. So it came as a bit of a shock at first.

Perhaps I am one of the last remaining anachronisms who is at all troubled by the likes of: 'In L8 17thC bills of xchange were issd by govt on a regulr basis as overcs trade xpnded.' Or 'The 4t of migratn to US attactd a gr8 % of servants and yng peple @ this time.' Or, my favourite to date, 'In Shxpeare's Eng u had 2 b rich 2 go to schl but sumX bys + grls lrnd reading and ritng at Om.'

Well, @ 1st i 4t, ang on a mo, wot is this? I cdnt bleve wot i was cing. NO! ?nt sumfing b dun? Thn it ht me: txt spk.

Text speak is now an established form of the written language. Apparently mobile phone owners fire off an average of eight text messages every day and by the end of 2004 we will have finger typed a total of 23 billion. We sent 85 million of them on Valentine's Day last month – 5 million more lots of 'i luv u' than on a normal day. So most young people, in particular, probably write more words in text English now than in standard English.

When set against this kind of abbreviated jargon the usual catalogue of colloquialisms or linguist errors in student work – split infinitives, the misuse of the apostrophe s, the difference between fewer and less, among other old favourites – are as nothing.

Regardless of the specific subject matter in question, one of the aims of formal education is still to develop the ability to produce written work that is grammatically and orthographically 'correct', as defined by authorised standards, and is suitably 'academic', as determined by the conventions of a particular discipline. What students who write in text speak fail to realise is that, in many contexts, the way in which they express themselves is at least as important as what they actually say.

The lingua franca of texting all goes to demonstrate the ancient theory that there is a high degree of correlation between the medium and the message. The vehicle of communication that we choose not only structures the content of what we say, but also the way in which we say it. We have one language for text and another for email, an English of the personal missive and another of the business letter, each of which has its own conventions and implicit understandings.

The problem comes when there is a mismatch between medium and message, as when text speak intrudes into academic essays, or informal usages are employed in formal documents. The fact that students are masters over the mechanics of new technology does not mean they have learned the rules of their various applications, which, although ever shifting, are still distinguishable. Just because text speak is quick to write does not mean it is acceptable in an exam script; simply because a senior professor is easy to contact by email does not mean that it is appropriate to address him or her as if they were an old mate.

At every major stage in the development of technologies of communication over the centuries, educationalists have worried about the effects that a new medium will have on the construction of knowledge, the form of its transfer and the mode of its expression. In Plato's *Phaedrus*, Socrates warns against the damaging effects the introduction of writing into the didactic process will have on the nature of oral exchange. With the advent of printing in Europe, scholars and churchmen noted the impact of the press in standardising written and spoken vernaculars. In the electronic age the language is patently evolving with a speed never before seen and some long-established rules or proprieties of its use appear under threat.

We can do nothing other than celebrate the inventiveness of which text speak is evidence. But as teachers we must insist that our charges learn to select that form of the written language, from the many now available to them, which is most suitable in the context. In a world in which standards of acceptable practice are being redefined at a bewildering rate, some lines have to be drawn in the sand and defended. Just a 4t.

Text: Building skills in English 11-14

Text 1

1 The writer of this article is a lecturer in a university. From the first paragraph:
   a How can you tell he is a lecturer or teacher?
   b How can you tell he is writing his article for other lecturers or teachers?

2 Why was the writer surprised to come across text speak in exam scripts?

3 Why do you think the writer uses figures like 85 million to support the point he is making in paragraph 5?

4 The writer makes two main points about written English in this article. Which two of the following statements best describe the points he is making?
   a Students must learn to produce work that has accurate spelling and neat handwriting.
   b What students write does not matter as much as the way they write it.
   c It is important that students learn to write standard English in school.
   d The way a text is written should match what the text is about and who it is for.
   e Text speak is quick to write so useful in examinations if time runs out.
   f Students should never use text speak because it is incorrect English.

5 In paragraph 10, why does the writer refer to different times in history?

6 The writer does recognise that there is a positive side to text speak. Write one quotation that shows his positive attitude and explain what he sees as positive about it.

7 How does the last paragraph of this text link back to the first paragraph?

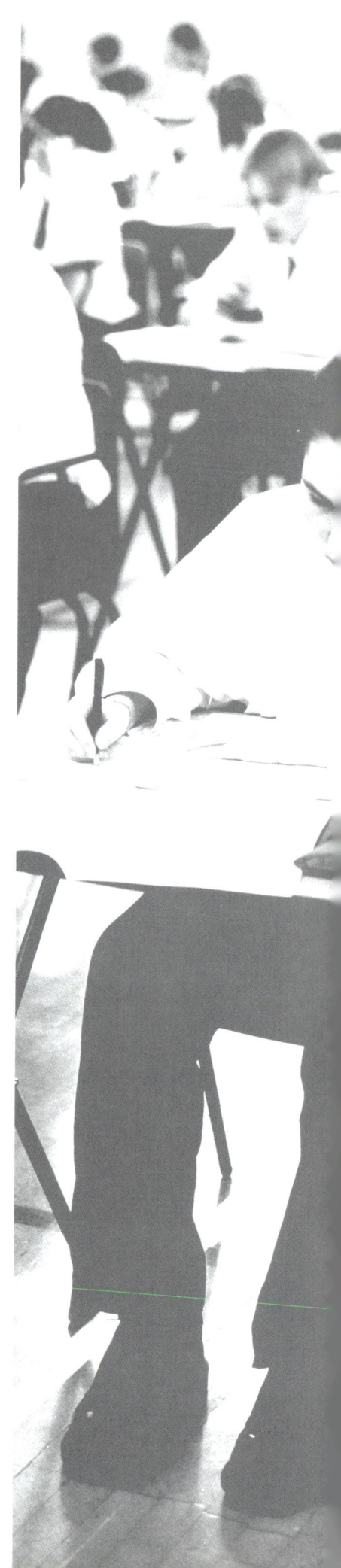

Text 2

www.teenagers_views.co.uk

Teenager's Views

News

Opinions

Entertainment

Sport

Features

Archive

| About | Contact | Links | Publish | Reporters |

Slang: The Good, the Bad and the Teenage

By Nicola Collins

30/6/2005

Being a 16-year old courageously fighting the mainstream has become increasingly easy since slang like 'phat' and 'mint' started to become prominent in today's teenage subculture. If you thought terms like 'neato', 'woop-se-daises' and 'super' were ridiculous well think again because there's a new wave of slang in town and it's taking the world by storm.

The term 'phat' isn't used for someone who is overweight but as a compliment meaning 'hip', 'cool' or 'trendy'. And 'mint' is no longer a sweet which freshens your breath but a term used to describe something which is flash and looks nice. Let's face it, trying to keep up with current slang (especially if you're an adult) is like trying to capture water in a sieve. The thing that really intrigued me though was where it all came from. Why do teenagers use it? I went on a mission to find out.

To my utter surprise, I discovered that people have actually written books and dictionaries to help understand slang. I knew the topic was serious, but surely not that serious.

In the 'Dictionary of Contemporary Slang', author, Tony Thorne, points out that slang changes so fast that only a proportion of it ever reaches any form of print, so the only way to capture it is to go out and listen for it. He also states that slang is used to provide a secret language, to a group or to mark some shared experiences, and at the same time excludes those who do not belong. In the tongues of criminals and teenagers, slang's main purpose is to provide a vocabulary that indicates one's inclusion in a particular group or exclusion from another.

That didn't surprise me at all. As a teenager myself, I have witnessed that including or excluding our peers is all we seem to be interested in these days and slang enables us to do this. Just say you're in the drama club at school. Only you and the others in the club are going to understand the lingo that you use when talking amongst each other. Anyone listening from the outside isn't going to understand what you mean when you say 'Well done Arthur, I thought your soliloquy in Act 1 Scene 4 was really moving' (a soliloquy, by the way, is a speech in a play that is meant to be heard by the audience but not by other characters on the stage showing the character thinking aloud). In the same sense, an adult isn't going to understand a group of teenagers talking about how 'mint' or 'phat' a car is at a car rally.

I'm now beginning to understand. Teenagers use slang to exclude adults from their conversations and ultimately their social lives. Maybe it's also a form of rebellion, a teenager's way of saying 'I don't like the way you're controlling me so I'm going to have conversations with my friends in a different language so I can have something that you don't control.'

I put my theory to Doug Martin, an English teacher with a Master's degree in linguistics. He thinks that using slang is part of a teenage rebellion that's been going on for years. 'I suspect it [slang] has been happening since cave-youth started grunting. In terms of it being rebellious or outrageous, of course it is. We tend to pick up on particular terms that we share in common which aren't shared with our elderly or with the much younger kids,' he said.

I actually have a theory of my own on where the term 'mint' originated from. Back in roughly 450BC the government building where money was made in Athens was called The Mint. See where I'm going with this? 'Mint' is a term used to describe something flash, flash things cost money, The Mint made the money. Maybe somewhere down the line someone picked up on it and turned mint into a popular teenage reference. Good theory right?

What I now understand about slang is that it's a natural thing for teenagers to do because it gives us some sort of a separate identity and it helps us in the age-old revolt against adults. The sad thing is it's going to be going on forever and nobody will be able to stop it. One thing's for sure, teenage slang is a phenomenon no one will ever understand.

Done

Text 2

1 What point is the writer making about new slang in the first paragraph?

2 'trying to keep up with current slang ... is like trying to capture water in a sieve...'
   a What does the phrase 'like trying to capture water in a sieve' suggest about keeping up with current slang?
   b Give another quotation from the last paragraph that repeats the same idea.

3 What two reasons does the article give for teenage slang? Do you agree with these reasons? Can you think of any other reasons?

4 What is the effect of including quotations from Tony Thorne and Doug Martin in this article?

5 In the last paragraph, the writer says 'teenage slang is a phenomenon no one will ever understand.' In what ways does this article suggest that this statement is true?

6 Look again at Texts 1 and 2.
   a Explain who you think the intended readers are for each article and why.
   b Now explain which of the facts or ideas in each article you found most interesting and why.

   Support your answer by referring to each article.

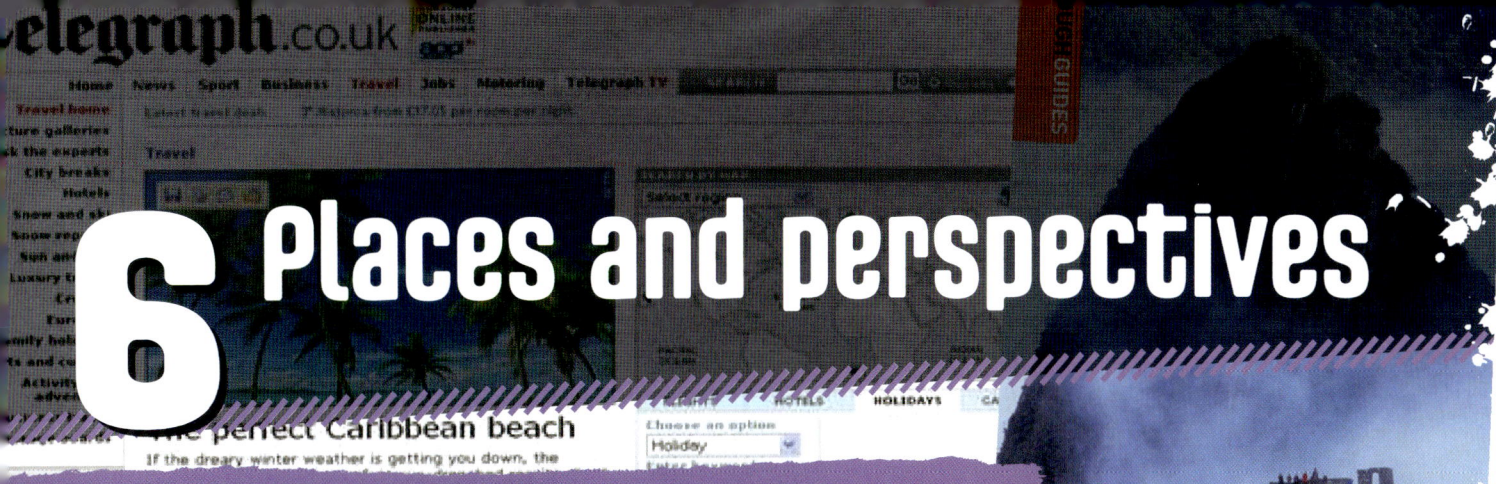

6 Places and perspectives

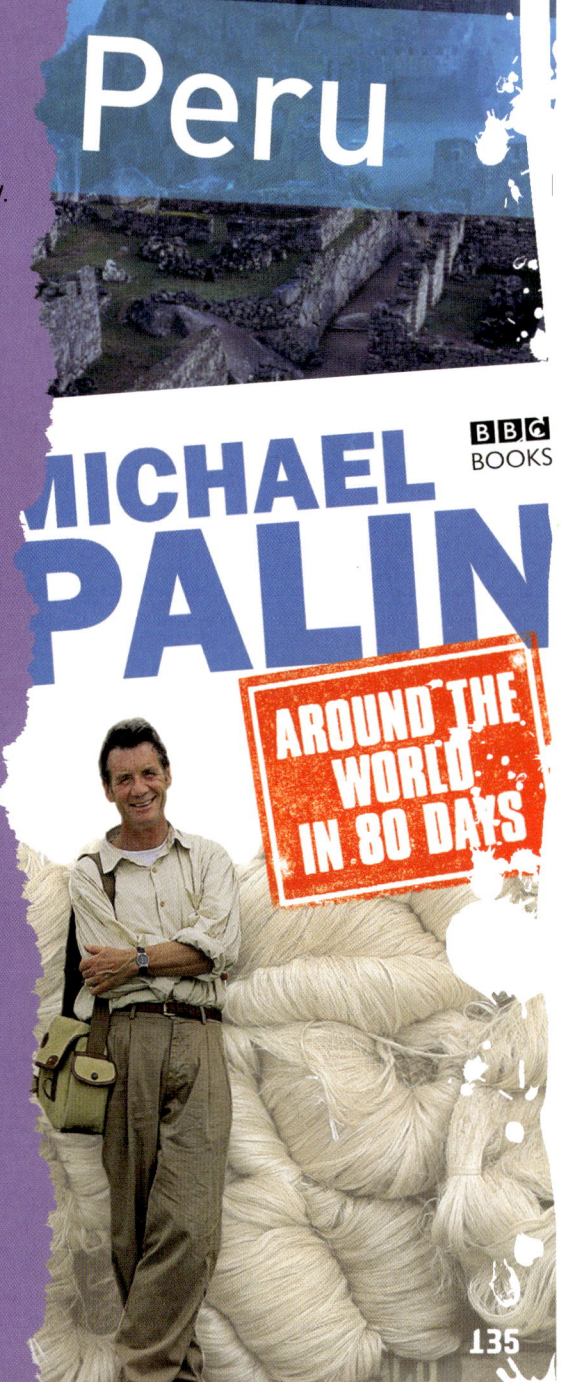

Objectives

In this unit you will:

Reading

- read a range of texts about travel writing and recognise their different purposes
- comment on how writers' language choices create effect
- infer how a writer feels about a place, both implicitly and explicitly.

Composition

- plan pieces of writing to meet a specific purpose
- write a range of texts, including recount texts and texts to inform and guide
- use adjectives and adverbs to create effective descriptions of places.

Speaking and Listening

- work in groups to discuss and solve problems.

By the end of this unit you will:

- complete two pieces of writing about a real place (Writing: Composition and conventions)
- take part in a group discussion (Speaking and Listening: Group discussion)

Cross-curricular links

- **Geography**
  Graphicacy and visual literacy – maps at a range of scales; Cultural understanding and diversity; Physical and human characteristics
- **Citizenship**
  Critical thinking and enquiry
- **History**
  Using evidence; Communicating about the past

1 What makes travel writing special?

You are learning:
- to understand the main features of travel writing.

Travel writing is always focused on a place, or the writer's experience of a place, other than home. The purpose of travel writing varies.
- Sometimes it is to *guide* others who might take a similar trip.
- Sometimes it is to *evaluate* a destination for possible visitors.
- On other occasions the purpose is to *share* an impression of a place or an interesting experience or journey.

Activity 1

Look at the following pieces of travel writing. Can you match them to the purposes described above?

Text 1

I arrived in Japan a dewy-eyed green sprout out of college, eager to devour a rich new culture and mingle with curious, exotic people. But after three months teaching in a smog-infested city near Tokyo, I was confronted mostly by other foreigners or garishly blonde Japanese bobbing their heads to Eminem, hypnotised by video games and fanatical about European labels. I couldn't help feeling that this wasn't the real Japan at all. Where was the land of the noble samurai, the whistling sakurabashis, the Zen harmony?

Text 2

Head back to the Jalan Raja, and veer left. You will come to the gleaming white Menara Dayabumi,with its fine filigree-like Islamic design. It is most impressive at night when its floodlit. Go past the general Post Office (open Mon–Fri 7.30a.m.–5p.m.) and take the pedestrian subway to the other side of Jalan Sultan Hishamuddin.

Text 3

If you're looking for the perfect way to have some serious fun and totally recharge, whatever the time of year, then look no further than Cornwall – it's a winner. The range of accommodation will suit almost any purse and any group; from extended families on a budget to honeymooners with no financial limitations! It's got it all: good food, great views and activities galore. The only thing you can't guarantee is the weather!

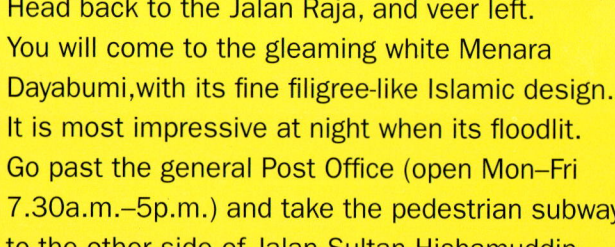

Text 4

The sea became green, the rocks all grey, and then, as I watched, the rim of the sun rose over the horizon and the sea held it as a scimitar of fire. The white disc rose, a miracle; it looked very large, as if it had grown bigger in the night. It paused a moment in the sea and then suddenly seemed to bound up from it: it flooded the world with light.

Activity 2

Each of the different types of travel writing is recognisable because of certain conventions, or special techniques, that the writers use.

1 Look at the list of writer's techniques below. Can you match them to the type of travel writing they are used in?

- use of comparatives (e.g. *bigger*) and superlatives (e.g. *most impressive*)
- emphasis on factual information such as opening hours
- focus on positive aspects of the place
- use of descriptive detail
- inclusion of web addresses and contact details
- matching of features of the place to the needs of travellers
- focus on the writer's feelings and actions
- inclusion of map references and directions
- discussion of positive and negative aspects of the place
- use of figurative language (words that paint pictures in your mind).

Use a table like the one below to record your ideas. The first technique has been inserted for you.

Type of travel writing	Writer's technique
Writing to evaluate	Use of comparatives and superlatives
Writing to guide	
Writing to explore an experience	

C
Each paragraph of my work concentrates on a specific aspect of a place, such as accommodation or things to see so that people can check out one thing at a time, or what's most important to them.

2 Travel writers also structure their work differently depending on the reason why they are writing. For examples read texts A–C.

Which structure best matches each type of travel writing in your table?

A
I usually structure my writing so that my readers can walk or drive and read as they get to each place.

B
Usually my stories have a chronological structure, although I do sometimes flash back or forward for effect.

Assess your progress

Write a definition of travel writing for an encyclopedia.

Which of the levels below do you think best describes what you have written?

Level 4	Level 5	Level 6
I can include the right kind of information and give some detail	I can use most of the right conventions for the form chosen	I can write convincingly in the style of an encyclopedia

2 Writing to inform and guide

You are learning:
- to write clearly about a place so that a visitor could be guided by your instructions.

One of the most common forms of travel writing is the guide-book or tourist information leaflet. They are written by 'experts' who either live in the country featured or have spent time getting to know it in order to pass on advice and tips. These types of guide are usually published as a book or an online resource. However, sometimes guides are written to lead visitors around a specific attraction and are only available once you get there.

Activity 1

1 Imagine that you are planning a trip to a city that you have never visited before.

Make a numbered list of all the questions you would find it useful to have answers to, in order to get the most out of your visit, such as:
- How can I get around the city?
- What sort of food is popular?

2 Now draw a timeline like the one below and place your questions on it, indicating when you would need to know the answer.

| 6 weeks before | 4 weeks before | 2 weeks before | on arrival | 1 week after arrival |

3 Now look at the contents page of the *Rough Guide to Iceland*

Why do you think the author has ordered their guide in this way? Would you change the sequence they have used?

CONTENTS

Introduction ix

Activity 2

Sometimes guide-books contain detailed instructions so that readers can navigate around an area or attraction.

1 Read this extract from *The Insight Pocket Guide to the Seychelles* and make a list of the words that tell you what to do. Can you follow the route on the map?

2 Write a paragraph guiding readers to the Victoria market. Start your directions like this:

'You should start your walk facing the...'

Test your instructions on a partner by getting them to trace the route on the map with their finger as you read it out to them.

Exit the gardens and turn left onto the main road and take the first turning off Le Chantier roundabout. This is Francis Rachel Street, which used to be the coastal road before the land to your right was reclaimed. The National Library is the big building to your right. Beyond it you will see the Cable and Wireless Building on the left. Look out for Kenwyn House, a traditional house owned by the company, set back from the road. A little further on the left, set well back, is Victoria's only mosque. Turn right just after this and park at the stadium car park.

Sharpen your skills Colons

Colons link two parts of a sentence. Writers of guide-books often use colons because they can be used to signal that more information is coming.

Link the first and second parts of the sentences below so that they make sense.

The town is full of places to go	:	fashion capital, home of the Duomo and the Teatro alla Scala.
You won't be able to resist the centre	:	'It's the city that never sleeps.'
No wonder they say	:	it's full of things to do.
Milan	:	parks, museums, cafés and galleries.

3 Recount writing

You are learning:
- to recognise recount texts and write your own.

Recount texts focus more on explaining a sequence of events than on describing where they happened, or how they made the writer feel. However, many recount texts are only interesting because of the unusual nature of the people, places and events they describe.

Activity 1

Recount texts have a predictable structure. They begin by telling the reader *who* was involved, *what* happened and *where* this event took place. This is called the **orientation**.

1   Read this opening of a recount text by Catherine Jones. Information telling you who was involved in the story has been highlighted.

In my early twenties, nervous with anticipation, I arrive by ferry in Messina. I travel armed with a long list of relatives to visit on my first trip to Europe – a trip that will plant the seeds for the many years I will live abroad. My mother and her brother, first-generation Americans, have written well ahead, and I am told that my numerous Sicilian kin eagerly await my coming. Drawn by a sense of both familiarity and mystery, I too impatiently look forward to meeting the characters of the colourful tales with which my effusive great aunt has regaled me.

Captured in time, like a Victorian watercolour, the villa of my Uncle Ivan sits on a cliff overlooking the bay at the edge of the town. The concierge admits me through a gate in a high stone wall abutting the street, to a vista of tiered gardens which slope, exactly as I have seen in old family photos, toward the iridescent blue and enigmatic sea.

Inside the white villa, a blue tile motif echoes the Mediterranean which can be seen through floor-to-ceiling windows. Ivan's wife welcomes me tightly to her bosom, but Uncle Ivan is chilly and straight-backed. Their two young children scamper among aunts, uncles, cousins, and curious neighbours.

2   Complete a spider diagram like the one on the right.

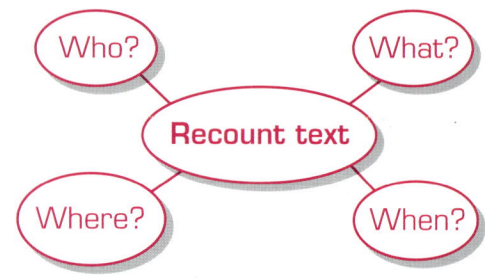

Activity 2

It is easy to recognise recount texts because they have a number of conventions:
- they focus on <u>individual people</u>, i.e. they use the words *I* or *we*
- they use words that indicate <u>when</u> (e.g. *before school*) and <u>where</u> the events took place (e.g. *outside the classroom*)
- they use words that <u>describe actions</u> (e.g. *helped, crushed*)
- they are often written in the <u>past tense</u>.

Read this second extract from Catherine Jones' recount. Does it follow the conventions listed above? Record your evidence as a bulleted list under the four headings: 'Individual people', 'When/Where', 'Actions' and 'Past tense'. Words showing focus on individuals have been highlighted.

Uncle Ivan and his wife are dressed in their finest black silk. A current of excitement sparks the air. The day appears to promise some big event. Under the strict command of my uncle, maids scurry about, placing flowers, zipping dresses, making me feel uncomfortable. Could I please dress for the occasion? I am asked. We are leaving soon for a restaurant. I am tired from travelling and unprepared for such brouhaha, but dutifully comply as best as I can.

Seated at the restaurant with my relatives and a bevy of their friends, I am confronted with a long table laid with every possible extraction of the Mediterranean, shelled and unshelled morsels, many of which I cannot identify by name, but that taste heavenly. And this is only the first course of seven. Repeatedly, I seem to be compared to my mother's mother. At least I perceive this as relatives pinch my cheek and recite my grandmother's name.

Upon returning to the villa, I am escorted to my room to nap by a maid who points to an adjoining villa, newly built in the same style. Another maid whisks into the room, cradling a white formal gown in her arms like a newborn babe. She seems to beg my opinion. The dress is beautiful. I express what I feel is a fitting 'Aah!' for such a fine gown, which elicits a relieved sigh from the maid, a sigh as heavy and warm as the sirocco wind sweeping in from Africa.

Here is the surprise ending of Catherine Jones' story.

Back home in the Midwest, I am to find out from my cousins that I have missed a wedding and caused what might be a permanent family rift. The next-door villa pointed out by the maid was built for the bridal couple. The bridegroom was a young, handsome, Italian doctor from my uncle's university. And the bride? It was to have been my wedding – unbeknownst to me, prearranged by my Sicilian relatives, in accordance with their tradition. Often, I will wonder who this bridegroom was, and if we would have lived happily ever after...

Activity 3

Write your own recount text, using the three-part structure, giving an account of an incident that took place somewhere away from home, when something unexpected or embarrassing happened to you or a family member. Check that you have used all of the conventions and an orientation and ending as discussed in this unit.

4 Descriptions

The purpose of some travel writing is to share the writer's impression of a place with the reader. The writer wants you to be able to imagine that you have been there too. To do this they use language and comparisons that appeal to all five of your senses.

Activity 1

1 Read this description of Tortuguero National Park in Costa Rica.

Costa Rica

Tortuguero National Park can only be reached by boat or plane. There are no roads in and no roads out. The journey by boat is slow and sometimes laboured as the thick red mud sucks at the underside of the boat and fallen trees partially block the way, grasping at the passing craft with blackened fingers. Yet rapidly you are transported back in time and the jungle noises begin to hint at dinosaurs lurking within.

Loud braying calls and sudden startling shouts from Howler monkeys set the vast, looming, cliff-like walls of many greens, rustling and wavering. Like heads of fresh broccoli the tree canopies cluster together, competing for light. Strings of creeper hang spaghetti-ish from the huge trees they are slowly strangling: mad maypoles without dancers. Startlingly, sudden licks of flame cut through the green: blood-red Heliconias, white-hot Ibis wings and the electric-blue Morpho. At ground level the tree trunks are ringed by thick buttresses: black rockets ready to launch.

Tiny beaches of grey sand are littered with huge ribcages: long-fallen tree canopies now bleached and brittle waiting to be swept away in the next tide.

The river below you is like hot chocolate, or sometimes cold, ebony coffee in the shady inlets where nobbly Caymen lurk just under the surface, floating like logs. Green river turtles float tantalisingly close, 'E.T.' heads bobbing up and back down, disappearing in the murky depths.

2 Make a table like the one below and fill in the first column with a list of all the nouns mentioned in the extract. Nouns from the first paragraph have been done for you.

Nouns	Adjectives	Adverbs
boat, plane, roads, mud, trees, craft, fingers, time, jungle, noises, dinosaurs		

   a Do these nouns give you a vivid picture of the park?

   b Now complete the next two columns of your table, adding all the adjectives and adverbs used by the writer. Is it easier to imagine the park now?

Activity 2

Writers spend a lot of time choosing the words that they will use so that all five of your senses are stimulated.

1 Draw a frame like the one on the right, then pick out 20 words from the extract and fit them into the correct area of the frame. Some words might fit into more than one category, in which case you can use the overlapping sections on the centre of the frame.

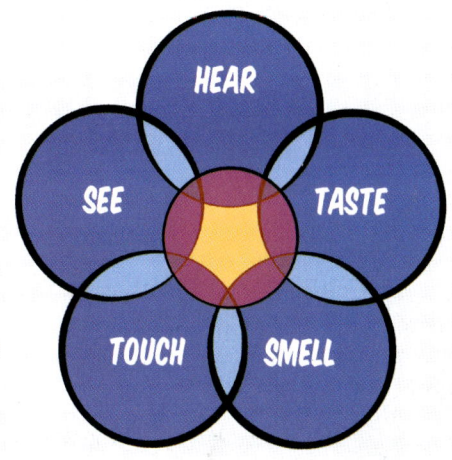

Activity 3

1 The writer compares the jungle scenery to several different things. Sometimes she uses similes:

'Strings of creeper hang spaghetti-ish'

'The river below you is like hot chocolate...'

and sometimes she uses a metaphorical sentence:

'...grasping at the passing craft with blackened fingers.'

Why do you think she chose these comparisons? Write down your ideas using the stem phrase:

'I think that she chose this comparison because it makes me think about...'

2 Can you make up four more comparisons that could be inserted into sentences in the passage?

   a Create two similes (remember: a simile compares two things using *as* or *like*).

   b Next, create two metaphorical sentences (remember: a metaphor is where you say that one thing is another.)

Activity 4

A description of a place is not complete unless the writer has suggested what the mood of the place is like. This is called the atmosphere.

Sometimes a writer will give you very obvious information about the atmosphere of a place. At other times you have to read between the lines, or deduce the atmosphere of the place.

1   a   Look at the annotations on this extract from the description of Tortuguero that you read earlier.

   b   Complete annotations 4, 5 and 6.

> 1 Not easy to get there... probably not many people... a lonely place.

> 2 It sounds like you'd be quite vulnerable as you couldn't escape fast... threatening place

> 6

Tortuguero National Park can only be reached by boat or plane. There are no roads in and no roads out. The journey by boat is slow and sometimes laboured as the thick red mud sucks at the underside of the boat and fallen trees partially block the way, grasping at the passing craft with blackened fingers. Yet rapidly you are transported back in time and the jungle noises begin to hint at dinosaurs lurking within.

> 5

> 3 'Sucks' sounds as if the mud is alive and trying to eat the boat... scary...and weird

> 4

2   Which one of the statements below best describes the atmosphere created by the description of Tortuguero? Why?

'It was a lively, exciting place to be.'

'It was tense and exciting.'

'It was quite a threatening, mysterious place.'

'It was a boring, dull place.'

Activity 5

1 Look at the photographs on page 142 and the one opposite. They are all taken from a boat travelling through Tortuguero.

   a You are going to write a description of each picture. Decide what sort of atmosphere you want to create in your description.

   b Write one paragraph about each one, using as many adjectives and adverbs, comparisons and atmospheric details as you can to create a multi-sensory image for your reader.

Assess your progress

Look at your descriptions of the photographs. Think about the words that you have used. Which of these statements best fits your work?

Level 4	Level 5	Level 6
I chose a few of the words because I knew that they would make my reader react	I chose most of the words because I knew that they would make my reader react in a particular way	I was really careful to match the words I used with the effect I wanted to create

Sharpen your skills Sequencing

1 An effective paragraph is one that contains sentences that are clearly grouped together for a reason. The writer of the description of Tortuguero decided to group her sentences by topic.

Each of the headings below summarises the content of one of the paragraphs. Put them in the correct order to match the sequence used by the writer.

   A The beaches   C The water

   B The journey into the park   D The appearance of the trees

2 Look again at the second paragraph of the extract about Tortuguero. Why are the sentences placed in this order? Are they:

   a placed in chronological order

   b ordered to build up extra details and examples of an idea

   c sequenced to suggest the writer's eyes moving around the scene?

5 Author's point of view

You are learning:
- to analyse how writers use language to express a viewpoint, their ideas and emotions about a place or an experience.

Travel writing is often very personal. As you have seen, some types of travel writing are focused entirely on an individual's experience of a particular place or journey. Other people might have a totally different time there, and might feel very differently, even if they were doing the same things.

Activity 1

1 Read this extract from a story posted on a website called 'Tales from a small planet', written by ten-year-old Magdalena Travis.

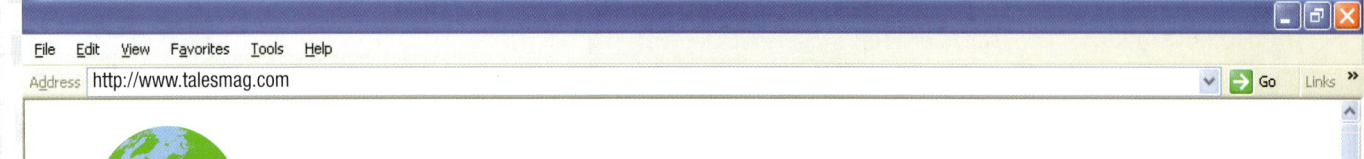

 # Tales from a small planet

In the summer of 2004, my family moved to Accra, Ghana. I was seven years old then. On the one hand, I did not want to say goodbye to my friends in Poland where my family and I had been living – my Dad works for the U.S. State Department and Krakow was our first post. On the other hand, I was curious: what would Africa feel like? My image of Africa was a big sand dune with elephants, giraffes and zebras, covered with plantain trees and coconut palms.

Well, this was one of the times when I was wrong. Accra is a busy town with dusty winds from the Sahara during the harmattan season. Over the two years I spent here, a great number of exciting things happened. In Mole National Park, I saw elephants roaming free and naughty baboons stealing crackers and bananas. I learned to boogie board and enjoyed many days on sandy beaches finding sea shells and sand dollars. If I was thirsty, I'd ask my Mom for a drink and, as unreal as it seems, she would say: 'OK dear, why don't you find a man with a machete to climb up a tree and get a coconut for you?' Fresh coconut juice was my favourite drink in Ghana. One time I met a great Ashanti chief and danced at the festival in his village. I also had a great experience attending Lincoln Community School, an international school uniting many cultures.

Normal days there were spent getting up at six-thirty, and then waiting for the bus to come between seven and seven-thirty. The bus would come at different times because of security concerns. I didn't like it, because you never knew if you'd be charging for the bus, or sleeping on it going home. Then we would go to school, eat a snack at nine, and eat lunch at twelve. We would come home on the bus (you were definitely not lucky if you were last to be dropped off!). On Saturdays and Sundays, my dad would pack us all in the car and we would be on our way to a beach. I would relax in the warm sand and then let the water carry me towards the waves on my boogie-board. However, there is something you need to watch out for on a Ghanaian beach. It is the outdoor, behind-a-rock-or-straight-on-the-warm-sand OUTHOUSE! It can really stink up the place.

Once I met some village kids on the beach. I thought they wanted to play, and they did for a while, although they could hardly speak English and we had to find other ways to communicate. However, when my Mom called me for lunch and I was walking away, they begged me for money and food. I did not know what to do so I just ignored them, but it pretty much ruined my day. But then I started thinking... Before I came to Ghana, I always thought everyone had the same amount of money. I soon came to learn that the world did not quite work in that way. This made my feelings mix and my stomach churn. I did not know quite what I was feeling. It was a mix of melancholy and fury. My mind was racing and for the first time in my life I realised that people were different not only by looks but by how much they had. Suddenly I thought the concept of money was not such a great idea after all. This feeling stayed with me for the rest of our tour in Ghana.

2 Sometimes writers are clear about their feelings about a place or experience; they even name them for us. Make a spider diagram like the one on the right, recording the emotions that Magdalena names in her piece of writing. You could add drawings or symbols to help you understand your notes later.

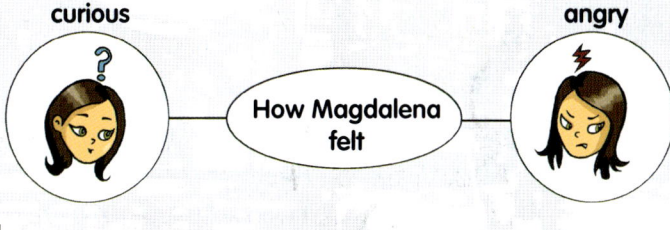

curious

angry

How Magdalena felt

3 The most effective pieces of writing usually present a clear reaction to a place. This helps to involve the reader, who usually wants to decide whether they agree or disagree. Magdalena's feelings at the start of her stay in Ghana are a little confused because she would rather not leave her friends, but once she settles down she clearly describes a consistent viewpoint about her new lifestyle.

a Complete a table like the one below showing her thoughts and feelings about Ghana.

Positives	Negatives
Unusual animals to see	

b Would you say that Magdalena felt:
- more positive than negative
- more negative than positive
- a constant mixture of the two?

Activity 2

1 Another way in which writers give us clues about their viewpoint is by using words that have precise meanings. These words give us an idea of what and how strongly the writer is thinking and feeling. For instance, when Magdalena says: 'It can really stink up the place' she could have used many other words instead of *stink*.

   a Jot down at least five other words that describe a smell.

   b Now put them into order, starting with the one that suggests that the smell is bad and ending with a word that suggests the smell is good. Where does *stink* fit into your rank order?

2 Look again at what Magdalena says about meeting the Ashanti chief.

   Think about the word *great*. Can you make a line of words that are similar in meaning and then use one in a sentence that would make your enjoyment seem even stronger than Magdalena's?

> 'One time I met a great Ashanti chief and danced at the festival in his village. I also had a great experience attending Lincoln Community School, an international school uniting many cultures.'

Activity 3

Writers can also make us guess how they are thinking and feeling about a place or experience. Sometimes we need to deduce or infer their ideas and emotions from the words and phrases that they use. One way of doing this is to try to unpick all of the ideas that a word puts into your mind. Imagine that the word is like the tip of an iceberg and under the surface are all the ideas that it puts in your head. Use these as clues to work out what the writer meant.

a For instance, how do you think Magdalena was thinking and feeling when she wrote 'unreal as it may seem' in paragraph 2?

b Now write a description of a place you really like, using some words that would give the reader a clear impression of your viewpoint. Use the writing frame below to order your thoughts.

_____ is a _____ place with so much to please. Starting with the _____ a visitor is quickly _____. Moving on to consider the _____ everyone is usually _____ by the _____ but if not then there's always the _____ to make you _____

'unreal'
magical
she's in awe
it wasn't what she was used to
amazing

Activity 4

The viewpoint of a writer can also be seen even when they are not writing in the first person. Charles Dickens and Wilkie Collins were famous Victorian writers who worked together to produce a story based on their walking tour of the English countryside. Their story is called *The Lazy Tour of Two Idle Apprentices*.

1 Read this extract.

> He kept it a secret; but he would have given a very handsome sum, when the ascent began, to have been back again at the inn. The sides of Carrock looked fearfully steep, and the top of Carrock was hidden in mist. The rain was falling faster and faster. The knees of Mr Idle – always weak on walking excursions – shivered and shook with fear and damp. The wet was already penetrating through the young man's outer coat to a brand-new shooting-jacket, for which he had reluctantly paid the large sum of two guineas on leaving town; he had no stimulating refreshment about him but a small packet of clammy gingerbread nuts; he had nobody to give him an arm, nobody to push him gently behind, nobody to pull him up tenderly in front, nobody to speak to who really felt the difficulties of the ascent, the dampness of the rain, the denseness of the mist, and the unutterable folly of climbing, undriven, up any steep place in the world, when there is level ground within reach to walk on instead.

Biography

Charles Dickens 1812–70
Charles Dickens is regarded as one of the greatest writers in the English language. He was acclaimed for his rich storytelling and memorable characters, and achieved worldwide popularity in his lifetime.

2 Which of the following statements best describes the authors' viewpoint in the extract and why?

a They thought that Mr Idle had a dreadful time and felt sorry for him.

c They found Mr Idle's over-reaction amusing and enjoyed remembering it.

b They found Mr Idle irritating because he made a lot of fuss about nothing.

Assess your progress

The table below shows you how to get better at showing your viewpoint in writing. How well are you doing?

Level 4	Level 5	Level 6
I can show one simple idea or attitude clearly and consistently through my writing	I can show a more complex idea in my writing	My viewpoint is consistent through my writing

6 Creating two different views of the same place

You are learning:
● to compare the writing of two different authors.

Different travel writers often visit the same places. However, they do not always give the same picture of the place, or of what they have seen and done.

Activity 1

Read these two descriptions of travelling in Patagonia, a desert-like area of southern Argentina.

Extract A: from the diaries of Lady Florence Dixie

After another day's sojourn at this encampment we resumed our journey. We took a good supply of fuel with us, as we were now entering on the barren, woodless region, during our transit over which we should have to rely solely on the provision we now made.

Leaving the beechwood behind us we rode up on to a plain, on whose edge we could distinguish what appeared to be a little black cloud. In reality it was a peak, or rather clump of peaks of the Cordilleras, at the foot of which we were one day to camp, and towards which for the next few days we directed our horses' heads.

This day's ride, and it was a long one, was by far more monotonous and dreary than any of the preceding ones. The immense plateau over which we rode for six or seven hours was remarkable for its gloom and barrenness, even in a region where all is sterility and dreariness. There was no sun, and the sky, lowering and dark, formed a fit counterpart to the plain, which stretched flatly away to the indistinct horizon, grey, mournful, and silent.

We could not help being affected by the aspect of the scenery around us, and I do not remember ever to have felt anything to equal the depression of spirits to which I, in common with all our party, fell a prey, and to whose influence even the guides succumbed.

Extract B: from *Argentina*, a book of photographs by Florian von der Fecht

Nature is the main character in Patagonia, one of Argentina's most imposing scenes. Its rugged beauty always resisted attempts of conquerors and settlers who intended to control it in order to extend their power. Only those who persevered with extreme courage and determination were finally able to inhabit these desolate lands. With enormous personal sacrifice, some people settled in the valleys surrounded by arid plateaux where no drinking water was available; others chose to stay close to the coast, in barren lands with no vegetation and putting up with very tough, cold winters. And the wind…always the wind with its devastating ways.
– 'Why then,' – Darwin wondered – 'do these arid lands possess my mind? Not only mine…I can't find a logical explanation but, in a way, I believe it may be because these lands widen the horizons of our imagination.'

Activity 2

Using the two extracts on page 150, copy and complete the table below with words or phrases that each writer uses to describe the different aspects of Patagonia.

	Extract A	Extract B
The size of the area		
The type of landscape		
The appearance of the land		
The amount of vegetation		
The amount of water		
The variety of experiences to be had		
The atmosphere		
The quality of light		
Colours featured		
Sounds heard		
The way people react to their surroundings		

Activity 3

1   Look at the list of statements below. Which ones express the viewpoint shown in extract A and which ones the viewpoint shown in extract B?

● Patagonia is boring
● the landscape is impressive
● life in this region is difficult
● there is not much to look at
● the size of this area is a key point
● the atmosphere is depressing
● this area brings out the best in people
● this area brings out the worst in people
● the place is lifeless
● this region stimulates the imagination.

2   Write a paragraph summing up how each writer feels about Patagonia. Use quotations to justify your opinions. Remember to explain how the words used affect your impressions.

Sharpen your skills Suffixes

A suffix is a group of letters added onto the end of a word. Sometimes they are added to a word that already makes sense on its own, e.g: peace + ful = peaceful

At other times the root word has to change, e.g: happy + ly = happily

Complete these pairs of sentences describing two viewpoints on the same place, using the roots shown in brackets and one of the following suffixes:
-ion -ly -ant -ful -less -able -ing -ent

1   a   London is a (beauty) city full of (grace) buildings and (please) views.
    b   London is a (disgrace) place: full of (forget) views and (abhor) buildings.

2   a   As I turned the corner my heart sank (rapid) and I realised it was (hope).
    b   Every twist and turn of the path set my heart (pound) with (anticipate).

7 Writing a travel article for a newspaper or magazine

You are learning:
- to write a travel article to recommend or review a destination.

Most weekly newspapers have a travel section. This contains advertisements for holiday companies, hotels and resorts as well as a range of articles. Some of these are designed to offer recommendations to would-be travellers.

Activity 1

1 Read this article from *The Sunday Times*.

Instant weekend: Palma

There's more to the Mallorcan capital than playing sardines on a beach – such as fine eating, galleries and hotels, writes Chris West

Why should I go? This year, 9m people will fly to Mallorca. The good news is that 8,999,998 of them will head straight for the beaches, leaving you free to enjoy a compact collection of museums, galleries, restaurants and suave hotels.

What do I do? A stroll along the waterfront gives you the best view of La Seu Cathedral – a central landmark, with the old city arranged around and behind it. Built in the French-Gothic style, it's huge, with an altarpiece and giant candelabras by Gaudi. Es Baluard museum, home to modern photography, ceramics and paintings (www.esbaluard.org), is pretty spectacular to look at, too – it was created by adding stark concrete walls to the remains of Palma's 16th-century ramparts. It has an excellent restaurant, Es Robost d'Es Baluard, serving new Mallorcan cuisine (9 Plaça Porta de Santa Catalina; 00 34-971 719609; £24pp). But if you're the kind of philistine (like me) who thinks that the best souvenirs come in 100%

cashmere, make for Jaume III, one of the main shopping broadways. From there, go south, for the modern Spanish giants Zara and Massimo Dutti, as well as interesting little boutiques.

Where should I eat? Go straight to La Boveda, a noisy and authentic tapas bar on Carrer Boteria (971 714863). For those really in the know, there's Bar España, at the corner of Carrer del Bane and Calle de Can Escursac, farther up the hill into the old town (no telephone – and beware, they stop serving tapas at 10pm).

Where do I stay? If you're into posing in rooftop pools and flopping on four-poster day beds, try the Puro Hotel (www.purohotel.com; doubles from £173). It also has a private beach, a short taxi ride out of town, with massages and yoga (Cala Estancia, Can Pastilla; 971 744744). For true sanctuary, Hotel Convent de la Missio (www.conventdelamissio. com; doubles from £156) is a converted convent building in the old town, with a more ethereal vibe.

How do I get there? There are flights to Palma from 22 UK airports. Airlines include Jet2 (0871 226 1737, www.jet2.com), bmibaby (0871 224 0224, www.bmibaby.com), easyJet (www.easyjet.com) and Monarch (0870 040 5040, www.flymonarch. com). Aer Lingus (0818 365000, www. aerlingus.com) flies from Dublin.

– Chris West travelled as a guest of the Spanish Tourist Office (020 7486 8077, www.tourspain.es).

1   The writer of this article uses a number of strategies to recommend Palma to the readers. Can you find examples of the following techniques in the passage?

- using comparatives and superlatives
- matching attractions to specific types of visitor
- using words with positive associations.

Here are some examples taken from the first paragraph:

- Comparatives: 'There's more to the Mallorcan capital than…'
- Superlatives: 'the best souvenirs'
- Matching attractions to specific types of visitor 'The good news is that 8,999,998 of them will head straight for the beaches, leaving you free to enjoy…'
- Using words with positive associations: 'compact collection of museums, galleries, restaurants, suave hotels.'

2   Imagine that your family wants to take a home-exchange holiday. Write a short article that could be used on a website to promote your home and its surroundings as a holiday destination. Start your entry:

> Welcome to your home away from home; it's got it all. For the comfort lover there is…

When you think you have finished, read it through and see if you can highlight examples of the three techniques that Chris West used. If not, add some!

Sharpen your skills Homophones

Homophones are words that sound the same but are spelt differently, e.g:

- there/their/they're
- new/knew
- your/you're
- whether/weather
- to/too/two
- past/passed

The best way to get them right is to learn what they mean and then work out which word fits where.

Proof-read this travel article and see how many homophone errors you can find. Be ready to explain why you think they are errors and to spell the word that should replace them.

I wasn't looking forward too my mid-week break in York, truth be told. It's chilly up their isn't it, and weather or not it rains is just a matter of time, I've heard. Someone at work had told me that York is big on Vikings, whatever that means! As soon as I arrived in the city I new I'd been wrong to wish myself sent elsewhere. The passed is everywhere you look: bits of ancient wall loom above you as you shop, Roman baths sit, empty and waiting, under your feet in the pub and ghosts lurk in every corner. Oh yes, and of course, the Vikings lie in wait two!

Assessment task

Writing: Composition and conventions

Machu Picchu – a place to visit?

Your task

Complete two different pieces of writing about a real place called Machu Picchu, using Texts A and B and the photos to help you.

1 The first piece of writing that you will complete is an extract from a tourist guide giving information about Machu Picchu.

Things you will need to think about in order to write an extract from a tourist guide:

- what information to select that is relevant for this purpose
- how you are going to organise this information effectively for a tourist guide
- how you are going to explain your ideas clearly for the reader
- what type of words and phrases this type of writing typically uses.

Machu Picchu, Lost City of the Incas, is an ancient city high in the Andes Mountains in Peru...

2 The second piece of writing is a description of Machu Picchu as if it was written by Hiram Bingham, the first person to discover the lost city of the Incas in 1911.

Things you will need to think about in order to write a description:

- the choice of detail and sensory words and phrases to make your description lively and interesting for the reader
- the thoughts and feelings to include to make your description convincing
- the way you are going to organise your description.

Why not make a checklist or spider diagram of your ideas?

I had entered the marvellous canyon of the Urubamba below the Inca fortress. Here the river escapes from the plateau by tearing its way through the gigantic mountains of granite...

Text A

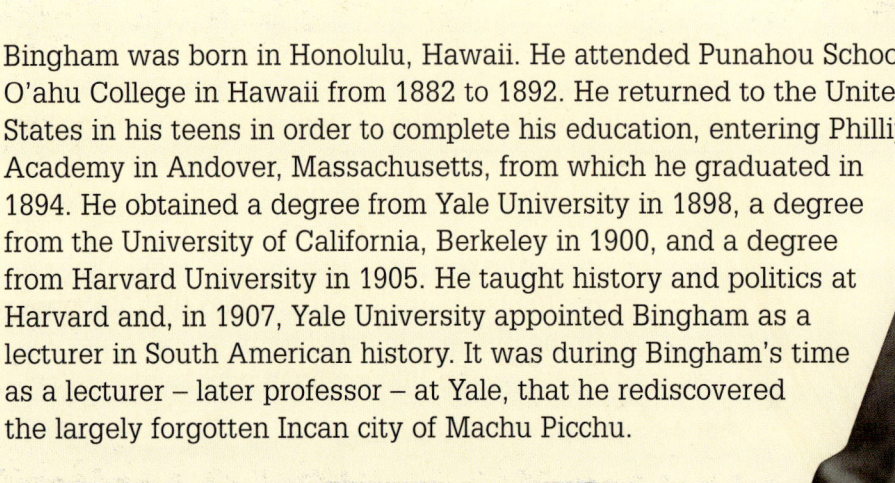

Bingham was born in Honolulu, Hawaii. He attended Punahou School and O'ahu College in Hawaii from 1882 to 1892. He returned to the United States in his teens in order to complete his education, entering Phillips Academy in Andover, Massachusetts, from which he graduated in 1894. He obtained a degree from Yale University in 1898, a degree from the University of California, Berkeley in 1900, and a degree from Harvard University in 1905. He taught history and politics at Harvard and, in 1907, Yale University appointed Bingham as a lecturer in South American history. It was during Bingham's time as a lecturer – later professor – at Yale, that he rediscovered the largely forgotten Incan city of Machu Picchu.

Here is some factual information about Machu Picchu that you could use in your writing. You could also do some further research using books and websites.

Text B

- Machu Picchu means 'old peak'.
- Machu Picchu was built between 1460 and 1470 AD by Pachacuti Inca Yupanqui, an Incan ruler.
- The city has an altitude of 8000 feet, and is high above the Urubamba river canyon cloud forest.
- Machu Picchu is a UNESCO World Heritage site.
- Machu Picchu has about 200 ruined buildings, mostly residences, although there are some temples, storage structures and other public buildings.
- Most of the structures are built of granite blocks. The blocks fit together perfectly without mortar, although none of the blocks are the same size and they have many faces; some have as many as 30 corners.
- Existing stone formations were used in the construction of structures; sculptures are carved into the rock; water flows through cisterns and stone channels; and temples hang on steep precipices.
- The city is surrounded by agricultural terraces that were sufficient to feed the population, and watered by natural springs.
- One of Machu Picchu's primary functions was that of astronomical observatory.
- The fauna in the reserve includes the spectacled bear, cock-of-the-rocks or 'tunqui', tankas, wildcats and an impressive variety of butterflies and insects unique to the region.
- It lies 43 miles northwest of Cuzco at the top of a ridge, hiding it from the Urabamba gorge below.
- It takes 3.5 hours by train and then a short bus journey to get to the city from Cuzco. There is also a helicopter service that drops people near the ruins.

Don't forget to produce a first draft of your two pieces of travel writing; then ask yourself whether you have used the correct conventions for each type of writing.

8 Organise a group presentation

You are learning:
- to work in groups to discuss and solve problems.

Doing anything in a group requires certain skills. Any decisions and actions will affect everyone. Does this mean that everyone has to have a say on every issue? How can disagreements be solved? What are the most important communication skills necessary for a good group discussion?

Activity 1

Read this transcript of an interview with 19-year-old student, Luke Picknett, about how he and his companions managed to work together to complete an exciting journey in the UK.

Interviewer: When you did the ten tors expedition on Dartmoor, was the group responsible for deciding the route that you would take and what you would pack?

Luke: We were told the ten tors that we were supposed to reach, then as a group of six we had to decide how we would actually get to them. We decided to divide up and take on certain roles. There was a leader and then two of us were in charge of navigation and then another two were in change of equipment and food. The leader had to make the final decision if we couldn't make up our minds.

Interviewer: Why do you think it was necessary to divide the work up like that?

Luke: Well, because it would have taken ages if we made all the decisions as a group of six. To be honest, some people don't really have a clue anyway, like, say, 'I can't cook so don't ask me what food to pack'! You have to give the right jobs to the right people.

Interviewer: Why do you think it would have been difficult if you had to confer with the whole group all of the time?

Luke: Because it would have caused arguments, it would have caused tensions, people would have had conflicting ideas and if you minimise that, it will make the whole expedition easier and the morale of the group better. But sometimes we did all discuss a decision – and then it's really important to listen to each other or you end up shouting! You also need to let everyone have their say, but not for too long, or people get stressy. At the end of the day the leader has to have the guts to say, 'That's it. I'm making a decision,' and everyone else has to live with it.

Imagine that you are designing an advice leaflet, 'Top Tips to Success when Planning in a Group'. Can you pick out any useful tips from the interview above? Write them down as a bulleted list, like the one that has been started for you below.

- Appoint a leader
- Make a plan

Activity 2

Now read this second extract, where Luke discusses another expedition, this time in Kenya.

Interviewer: There must be a lot of preparation for these trips and quite a bit of packing. How do you go about knowing what you need to take and making sure you've got the right things with you?

Luke: I made a list of the equipment I thought I would need. First of all I thought about the fact that I was going to a hot country, and divided all of my equipment down into categories, for example sleeping equipment and then clothing (which was quite difficult because I had to take clothing that would be relevant for a climb up a mountain but also for an equatorial climate, so I had to make sure that I packed shorts and thermals). I had to take into consideration the fact that I'd be carrying my stuff everywhere, so I tried to make it as lightweight as possible.

Interviewer: And did you ever take something that was totally inappropriate or see anybody with things that were just not right for the setting?

Luke: Well, one of the girls on the Kenya expedition took some hair tongs out with her, which was totally ridiculous. Obviously there's no electricity up a mountain – so she wouldn't be able to use those – ever.

Interviewer: So you've got to consider what the facilities are where you're going?

Luke: Yes, and the environment you're going to be living in and the things you'll be doing. That's really important so that you know what's appropriate to take with you.

Interviewer: You've done a lot of travelling, so how do you decide how you're going to get from A to B, or do you just always walk?

Luke: Definitely not, there is a public transport system in Kenya and it depends entirely on where you're going and how much time and money you've got. The most popular is a small mini-bus which seats 14 and they're very fast but they're also really dangerous, and then there are big coaches that are slightly more expensive. So, for example, when I was working for the charity, it was important to me to get round as cheaply as possible, so I would choose the option of the minibus despite the fact that it was dodgy.

Interviewer: Right, OK, but were there practical issues, like you couldn't take your luggage on a particular form of transport?

Luke: Yes, for example, on the minibuses it would be very uncomfortable – though it would be possible – to travel with all of your equipment, so you have to take that into account.

Assess your progress

Level 4	Level 5	Level 6
I can see that it is important to listen and respond to what others say in a discussion	I can see that I should try to build on others' ideas and respond to them in a discussion	I can see that I need to be sensitive towards other group members and begin to try to evaluate their contributions

Assessment task

Speaking and Listening: Group discussion and interaction

Expedition to Machu Picchu

Your task

Your school has been awarded a grant to organise a student expedition to Machu Picchu, with one condition: that the students organise the expedition themselves.

There are two key stages to this expedition:
1 Planning
2 Travelling

Stage 1: Planning

First, you have to decide who is going to be the scribe for this stage of the expedition. Their job is to record ideas, manage time and record any decisions made.

Your group needs to decide what to take with you. It's important to travel light, as the expedition will include some strenuous hiking. Look at the list of items below and discuss which are:

- Essential – it's vital that these items are be taken on the expedition
- Nice-to-haves – it would be nice to take these items, but the group could manage without them
- Irrelevant – these items serve no useful purpose on this expedition and should not be taken.

Remember to:
- explain your ideas as to why you think an item should or should not be taken
- listen to the ideas of others.

Stage 2: Travelling

- Sun cream
- Basic first aid supplies
- Comprehensive first aid supplies
- Walking boots
- Flip flops
- Cooking stove
- Swimming trunks
- Camera
- Water purifying tablets
- Camcorder
- Compass
- Guidebook
- Umbrella
- Phrase book
- Emergency rations
- Mosquito spray
- Sunglasses
- Hat
- MP3 player
- Towel
- Sleeping bag
- Waterproof clothing
- Rope
- Mobile phone
- Laptop
- Nintendo DS
- Thermals
- Hair dryer
- Mirror
- Firelighters
- Guide to dangerous jungle insects

During this stage, a number of things are going to happen to you as you travel. You have to decide how you are going to deal with each of them so you can move on successfully. Choose a scribe for this stage of the expedition.

You need to discuss and agree a solution to each of the problems, the scribe has to write it down and then you can move on to the next problem. Try to get through all of the problems before your time runs out.

- A member of the team sprains their ankle and can't walk.
- A member of the team drops their passport into the fast-flowing river.
- Ants eat all the fresh food.
- One of the group is exhausted and can't carry all of their equipment.
- The guide you were expecting is not at your agreed rendezvous point when you arrive there.

Peer-evaluation

Now you need to decide how well you worked as a group and as individuals within that group. You have to decide on a set of criteria by which to judge everyone in the team. Make a list of the skills and qualities that were useful in this assessment task. For example:

- listened to other people's ideas
- made useful suggestions.

Make a table like the one below, writing these criteria as headings along the top of the table and the names of your group members down the first column.

	Took a role and stuck with it	Made useful suggestions	Listened to other people	Encouraged other people to make suggestions
Jo				
Urvashi				

Next, ask yourself whether you showed those skills and qualities during this task. Give yourself a rating from 1 (a little) to 3 (a lot). Ask everyone in the group to rate you, so that you get a realistic overview of your contribution.

Heinemann is an imprint of Pearson Education Limited, a company incorporated in England and Wales, having its registered office at Edinburgh Gate, Harlow, Essex, CM20 2JE. Registered company number: 872828

www.heinemann.co.uk

Heinemann is a registered trademark of Pearson Education Limited

Text © Pearson Education Limited 2008

First published 2008

12 11 10

10 9 8 7 6

British Library Cataloguing in Publication Data is available from the British Library on request.

ISBN 978 0 435579 79 1

Designed and produced by Kamae Design, Oxford
Original illustrations © Pearson Education Limited 2008
Illustrated by Paco Cavero, Majorie Dumortier, Tony Forbes, Paul McCaffrey, Jo Tayor and Rory Walker
Cover design by Pete Stratton
Picture research by Caitlin Swain
Cover illustration by Andrew Painter
Printed in China (CTPS/06)

Acknowledgements

The author and publisher would like to thank the following individuals and organisations for permission to reproduce photographs:

Action Plus p9; Advertising Archives p5 (top and bottom); Alamy Images/ Elizabeth Whiting & Associates p58 (bottom); Alamy Images/ eye-D Prod pp88, 89, 90; Alamy Images/ Laurie Strachan p136 (top right); Alamy Images/ Martin Mayer pp131, 132 Alamy Images/ Travelib UK p56; Alamy Images/ Visual Arts Library, London pp 109, 114 (top left and bottom right); Bridgeman Art Library pp62, 63, 120 (top and bottom); Bridgeman Art Library/ Royal Society of Arts, London, UK p93; Caves of Lascaux, Dordogne, France/ The Bridgeman Art Library p110; Corbis p102 (right); Corbis/ Ashley Cooper p136 (bottom left); Corbis/ Bettmann p154 (bottom); Corbis/ Bob Krist p142 (top); Corbis/ Chris Hellier p149; Corbis/ Colin McPherson p40; Corbis/ Daniel Dal Zennaro/ EPA p94; Corbis/ Dennis Stone/ Elizabeth Whiting & Associates p59 (top); Corbis/ Francesc Muntada p150 (bottom); Corbis/ Gary Braasch p145; Cornstock Images p105; Digital Vision p60; FK Photo/ Corbis p66; Getty Images/ David Silverman p111 (top middle); Istockphoto pp 58 (right), 83 (top right and bottom), 84 (top), 111 (top right), 123 (top), 135 (bottom right), 138 (top, middle and bottom), 154 (top), 156; Kobal Collection/ New Line Cinema p34 (top); Kobal Collection/ Lake Film pp46, 48; Mary Evans Picture Library p150 (bottom); Moviestore Collection Ltd. p39; PA Photos p111 (top left); PA Photos/ Peter Jordan/ PA Archive p125; Pearson Education Ltd. Steve Shott 2006 p103; PhotoDisc p102 (left); PhotoDisc. Sexto Sol. Adalberto Rios Salía pp155, 158; PhotoDisc. StockTrek pp95 (bottom), 98; Photos 12/ Alamy p112 (bottom); Photolibrary p136 (top left); Popperfoto/ Alamy p62 (top); Redferns/ Paul Bergen p101; Redferns/ Alastair Muir p36; Rex Features/ Brian Rasic p101; Redferns/ Brigitte Engl p100; Rex Features/ C. S. Goldwyn/ Everett p44; Rex Features/ Image Source p120 (bottom); Rex Features/ Mark Obstfeld p84 (bottom); Rex Features/ NCUPHOTOBANK p42 (top 3); Rex Features/ Roger-Viollet pp114 (bottom left), 118; Still Pictures/ Chlaus Lotscher p142 (bottom); Topham Picturepoint p59 (bottom); Topham Picturepoint/ ArenaPAL/ Nigel Norrington p55; Topham Picturepoint/ Universal Pictorial Press Photo p42 (bottom).

Every effort has been made to contact copyright holders of material reproduced in this book. Any omissions will be rectified in subsequent printings if notice is given to the publishers.

Page from Cadbury World leaflet. © Cadbury World. Reprinted with kind permission; Beanz Meanz Heinz advert. Reprinted with permission of H. J. Heinz Company Limited; Oxy advert 'Zitty to Pretty' Copyright © The Mentholatum Company 2007. Reprinted with kind permission; Screenshot from www. centerparcs.co.uk. Reprinted with kind permission of Center Parcs Limited; Use of text and photographs regarding 10k run for Cancer Research. Reprinted with the kind permission of Cancer Research UK; Use of After Eights bags advert. Reprinted with permission of Société des Produits Nestlé S.A.; Use of homepage from www.wickedwomenchoppers.com. Reprinted with kind permission of Christine Vaughn; Use of homepage of www.chillisauce.co.uk. Reprinted with kind permission; Homepage from www.drivingmissdaisy.net. Reprinted with kind permission; Homepage from www.sheilaswheels.com. Reprinted with kind permission; Use of 'Best of Witney' postcard. Reprinted with kind permission; Extract from The Tulip Touch: a Play by Anne Fine and Rachel O'Neill, published by Collins Educational. Reprinted with permission of David Higham Associates Limited; Front Cover and small extract from The Tulip Touch by Anne Fine (Hamish Hamilton 1996) Copyright © Anne Fine 1996. Reprinted with permission of Penguin Group UK; Extract from Keeper by Mal Peet published by Walker Books. Copyright © 2003 Mal Peet. Reprinted by permission of Walker Books Limited, London SE11 5HJ; Extract from The Complete Fawlty Towers by John Cleese and Connie Booth. Copyright © John Cleese Connie Booth, Waterfall Production Ltd, 1977, 1979, 1988. First published by Methuen in 1988. Reprinted with permission of David Wilkinson Associates; Extract from Our Day Out by Willy Russell. Copyright © Willy Russell. Published by Methuen. Reprinted with permission of A&C Black Publishers; Use of extract of transcript from Only Fools and Horses Christmas Special. By John Sullivan. Reprinted with the kind permission of John Sullivan; Extract from Gregory's Girl by Bill Forsyth, published by Cambridge University Press. Reprinted with permission of Cambridge University Press and the author; Extracts from www.historybytheyard.co.uk reprinted with permission; Cover of Carol Vorderman's Massive Book of Sudoku by Carol Vorderman, published by Ebury Press 2005. Reprinted with permission of The Random House Group Limited; 'Split Personality' by Mark Turner, from World's Shortest Stories edited by Steve Moss. Copyright © 1998, 1995 Steve Moss, published by Running Press Book Publishers. Reprinted by permission of Running Press, a member of Perseus Books Group; 'Twenty rules for writing detective stories' by S. S. Van Dine, first published in American Magazine, September 1928. Reprinted with permission of The Marton Agency, New York; Short extract from A Pocketful of Rye (1953) © Agatha Christie Ltd, A Chorion Company, all rights reserved; Short extract from 'Shatter Proof' by Jack Ritchie originally published in Manhunt October 1960. Reprinted with permission of Sternig & Byrne Literary Agency on behalf of the Estate of Jack Ritchie; Short extract from A Murder is Announced (1950) © Agatha Christie Ltd, A Chorion Company, all rights reserved; Short extract from Three is a Lucky Number (1969) © Rights Ltd, A Chorion Company, all rights reserved; Short extract from Devices and Desires by P. D. James. Reprinted with permission of Greene & Heaton; Extract from Fire Sale by Sara Paretsky, published by Hodder & Stoughton. Reprinted with permission of Hodder & Stoughton and David Grossman Literary Agency; Use of page from www.facebook.com reprinted with permission of the page owners and Facebook; Crown copyright material is reproduced with the permission of the Controller of HMSO; Article 'Family: She's 14, looks 18, and is full of attitude…' by Sophie Radice, The Guardian, 20 October, 2007. Copyright © Guardian News & Media Limited 2007. Reprinted with permission; Extract from Moby's journal. www.moby.com/journal. © Moby. Reprinted with permission of Moby c/o DEF Management; Use of Steve Alton's blog. Copyright © Steve Alton. Reprinted with the kind permission of the author; Use of screengrab from www. logo.com © Logotron Limited. Reprinted with permission; Extract from NASA website. Copyright © NASA. Reprinted with permission; Use of screengrab from www.glastonburyfestivals.co.uk. Reprinted with kind permission; Extract from Remotely Controlled by Dr. Aric Sigman, published by Vermilion. Reprinted by permission of The Random House Group Limited; Extract from Slam by Nick Hornby, (Puffin Books 2007) Copyright © Nick Hornby 2007. Reprinted with permission; Chat with John Simpson from www.wordsmith.org. Copyright © Wordsmith. Reprinted with kind permission; Article 'Academic Text' by Adam Fox, The Guardian 17 March 2004. Copyright © Adam Fox 2004. Reprinted with kind permission of the author; Nicola Collins 'The Good, The Bad, and the Teenage' © Nicola Collins. From www.barbedwire.com; 'A Brief History of Cool' (graph) Fast Company Magazine, issue 107, July 2006. By Fast Company Staff. Copyright 2006 by Mansueto Ventures LLC. Reproduced with permission of Mansueto Ventures LLC via Copyright Clearance Centre; Extract adapted from Anancy and Bredda Lion from www.jamaicans.com reprinted with permission; Front cover from Rough Guide to Peru 6th Edition, by Dilwyn Jenkins (Rough Guides 1997, 2006) copyright © Dilwyn Jenkins 1992, 1997, 2006. Reprinted with permission of Penguin Group UK; Page from Telegraph holiday online. Reprinted with permission of Telegraph Media Group; Front cover from Around the World in 80 Days by Michael Palin published by BBC Books. Reprinted with permission of The Random House Group Limited; Contents page from Rough Guide to Iceland 3rd edition (Rough Guides 2001, 2004, 2007) Text Copyright © David Leffman and James Proctor 2001, 2004, 2007. Reprinted with permission of Penguin Group UK; Extract and map from Insight Pocket Guide to the Seychelles. Reprinted with permission of Insight Guides; Runaway Bride by Catherine Jones, from Tales from a Small Planet. Reprinted with permission of Tales from a Small Planet and the author; Extract from a story by Magdalena Travis from www. talesmag.com Reprinted with permission; Extract from Argentina by Florian von der Vecht. Reprinted with permission of the author and D. G. Ana Victoria Vergeli Photo Design Argentina; Article 'Instant Weekend: Palma' by Chris West, Sunday Times, September 23rd 2007. Copyright © NI Syndication Limited 2007. Reprinted with permission.